The Faultless Imperfection

The United States Constitution Revisited
A citizen's view of a revered document

by

James F. Oshust

Putting our Constitution back where it belongs:
into the hearts and minds of all Americans,
and in the classroom

Leicester Bay
BOOKS

Newport, Maine

Leicester Bay Books
First Edition(CS) – First Printing 2017
ISBN 13: 978-1979094405
ISBN 10: 1979094403
Kindle Edition: 2017

Leicester Bay Books
PO Box 536
Newport, Maine 04953-0536

www.leicesterbaybooks.com

Disclaimer:

This work is the writer's personal evaluation and commentary related to the wordage and structure of the Constitution, drafted in September 1787 and as expanded by Amendments to this current time. I have particularly subdivided several of the Amendments so as to highlight and bring specific attention to individual commentary. As is with any such a document, subject to the vagaries of ongoing discussion and counter proposals, it is left to agreement or dispute by readers. An endowed right as encompassed in the document itself. It should be noted that some of the spellings appear to conflict with current usage but are presented reflecting the actual printing and language in use at the time of the original document. The writer offers no claim of academic expertise or extensive resources for the personal observations contained herein. With all due respects to those who will disagree, I have attempted to bring a sense of balance in the thinking for the benefit of anyone taking the time to read the Constitution. We are constantly besieged by those desiring immediate change that we must evolve in the interpretation the original wording and change that which is no longer relevant in their opinion, much as mankind has evolved. Yet that evolution was the result of millennia of change to meet need, recognition of required servicing of the ability to survive. Should we not now be more circumspect in making those requested or demanded changes?

The views of the author are not necessarily the views held by the publisher, who does represent, however, the author's right to his opinion and his right to state that opinion in print and publicly.

Dedication:

This volume is dedicated
to those Americans whose service and sacrifice
was willingly spent to assure its preservation
over the years of our nation's history.

Table of Contents

●●●

Prologue

"Let every American, every lover of liberty, every well-wisher to its posterity swear by the blood of the Revolution never to violate in the least particular the laws of the country, and never to tolerate their violation by others. As the patriots of `76 did to support the Declaration of Independence, so to the support of the Constitution and laws, let every American pledge his life, his property, and his sacred honor. Let every man remember that to violate the law is to trample on the blood of his father and to tear the charter of his own and his children's liberty. . . Let it be taught in schools, in seminaries, and in colleges, let it be written in primers, in spelling books, and in almanacs, let it be preached from the pulpit, proclaimed in legislative halls, and enforced in courts of justice. And, in short, let it become the political religion of the nation, and in particular, a reverence for the Constitution."

– Abraham Lincoln

"The people made the Constitution, and people can unmake it. It is a creature of their own will, and lives by their will" John Marshall, Chief Justice of the U.S. Supreme Court (1755-1835)

Personal observations of a document dearly held vital to the freedoms of those who would read this treatise.

● ● ●

Preface

Preamble to the United States Constitution

"We the People of the United States, in order to form a more perfect union, establish justice, insure domestic tranquility, provide for the common defence, promote the general welfare, and secure the blessings of liberty to ourselves and our posterity, do ordain and establish this Constitution of the United States of America."

COMMENT: Since its inception, The United States Constitution has been the subject of millions of pages of opinion, interpretation and academic punditry. "The Faultless Imperfection" attempts to present the entirety of the prefacing articles, the original documents wording and its later amendments. In each section, specific references and individual allowances or prohibitions are discussed – from an average citizen's viewpoint – without the semantic soliloquies so apparent in all those past tomes produced by those who either seek to restate or reduce the contents of those cherished documents. To add fuel to the dying embers of understanding of the Constitution by our younger generation, the addition of numerous suggestions and possible revised language is discussed. More importantly discussed is the emphasis on the need to become reasonably familiar with this instrument of our founding. The work is intended for John/Jane Q. Public, and hopefully their children. As their parents become aware of the paucity of any formal education on the subject – once a required subject in schools which has gone the way of other subjects considered either irrelevant in today's highly mobile society, or discarded as a necessary loss to make way for instruction in the modern, more liberal oriented curriculum – maybe they/we will be motivated to spearhead a return to a study of the Faultless Imperfection of the Constitution of the United States in our minds and in our schools.

● ● ●

The Beginning

"We hold these truths to be self-evident, that all men are created equal, that they are endowed by their creator with certain inalienable rights that among these are Life, Liberty and the pursuit of Happiness."
 – (the second paragraph of the

Declaration of Independence – July 4, 1776)

COMMENT: The American Revolution was not what the colonists actually intended. A revolution, as the standard meaning would imply, is to overthrow what exists. It was not the aim of those who initiated the first rebellious actions. They were wholly concerned with separating themselves and their yet unaware constituency from the yoke of King George and the entire English domination. Their goal was not the overthrow of the monarchy. Rather, to be allowed, without interference or over sight by any foreign power, to govern themselves in a manner that would be constructed and function free of beholding to any other influence. It was through this upheaval and eventual release by the English royal house that a new nation was formed. One that was especially unique in the history of the world and became a beacon of desired freedom by so many others throughout the globe for years to come. To encompass that new sense of individual liberty and self-determination, there needed a written dialogue, a charter of those rights and sovereignty to assure what had been formed would survive and remain the protected covenant of all its inhabitants. Thus the creation of the United States Constitution, a document revered, yet remaining the center of controversy among those who view it as either a near biblical tome, or those who feel it is a living document subject to change as social commentary might dictate.

● ● ●

From Hope to Reality

The United States Constitution, from its inception, its original design and throughout its nearly two hundred and thirty years, has remained a symbol of personal and societal freedom to all those across the globe seeking release from tyranny and deprivation of the human expression they have too long and too often been denied. It is the matrix of the finest governmental structure ever devised. Yet, as one must quickly recognize, it was the result of human consideration and compromise, every facet dependent on the foibles of a flawed mankind. A human species that since the beginning of time has exhibited both brilliance and flawed perception, too often in conflict one with another. The Founding Fathers sought to create a government that truly emphasized the participation of each and every citizen; one which allowed access to our liberties and benefits through a specified and welcoming process; a process that enabled so many of our ancestors the opportunity to achieve what the tyranny, disallowance and institutional poverty that constantly restrained the human spirit's desire to gain a rightful place in society. The Founders strived to articulate a form that would protect the individual and the body of government as an effective administration for the sole purpose of the good of the people it served. To allow both the private citizen, and his or her elected officials, to pursue those methods and efforts required to withstand any deterioration of those rights along with the incursion by foreign forces or influences.

Deceased U.S. Supreme Court Associate Justice, Antonin Scalia, is reported to have asked if the present Constitution, as now existing, is any longer a valid document. Inasmuch as the Constitution is recognized as the "Law of the Land", we face a conundrum. The law, as we know it, is the adhesive assuring that the fragile fabric of our national structure, woven in the name of individual rights, remains intact; that it will not fray any more, even through its careless handling by our political leadership and national administration.

To clarify history, this is actually the second constitution. The first document being the Articles of Confederation which permitted and occasioned what might be referred to as a de facto government. Formulated in 1777, it authorized raising and financing an army in the struggle to gain separation from England. Furthermore it entitled the new organization the right and privilege to invite and deal with diplomatic agents and to enter into treaties with foreign governments. In reading the original Articles of Confederation one recognizes three major variances to what is now our functioning document. First, all matters dwelled in one legislative chamber called the Congress. Secondly, the authority of this early Congress did not stem from the people as a whole but rather from the original colonies/states. Third, matters decided or requested by that Congress were transmitted to the states for action including the imposition of taxes and the often controversial question of jurisdiction relating to legal matters and any type of criminal code. Very simply there was no national administration or central government as it were. In 1787 that all basically changed with the drafting of what we now accept as the United States Constitution.

Allow me to again emphasize that this is presented as one person's view of an admirable document. The reader must understand that the original articles and accompanying First Ten Amendments were the profound beliefs of the framers of the Constitution as to what type or form of government might provide the guarantee and protections of the citizenry as was considered worthy of consideration at that time. Although it disallowed several distinct racial, ethnic and economic classes at that time the document reflected what these Founding Fathers must have felt best fit the needs of the then majority based on their personal social, economic, political and more succinctly their particular religious and/or philosophical background and experience.

The offering of an average citizen with no legal training but an avidity for discussion and accelerated viewpoints of the Constitution, and is not meant as an instructive tool or scholarly description. There are many members of academia and historical research who can and have imparted their enlightened review of this document. Practically speaking, so many of our current laws were written for a different time and under different conditions. The society of man and its prevailing ethical and moral judgments were tempered by a desire to attend to whatever religious or moral belief that held sway at the time of the original writing and later amendments. We tend to judge today's differing opinion of certain parts of the constitution within the shadow of our present thinking and the ever evolving concept of personal freedom and individual expression. Time will always reflect growing and changing interpretations of the will of the public as opposed to the viewpoint and commitment of those in power. It is to the extent of such divergent considerations that this dissertation is presented. To forestall change or alteration or abuse that can forever deny the original intent of the document.

I cannot determine, nor rationally can anyone however erudite or highly trained in such, what our Founding Fathers intended or the social climate when they delved into certain aspects of individual, states and/or national rights. What I have written herein is first an observation of each section or individual part of the document. Then, where, I, as just an average citizen, find difficulty with the use, interpretation or current misuse of its language, I will be direct in my comments and suggest alternative or supplemental language or opposition—again my personal viewpoint. Readers will note that at times I merely recite certain sections, having no reason to suggest another approach due to lack of appropriate or sufficient reasoning for any suggested change or alteration.

Furthermore it need be understood that the underlying principles of our current Constitution were not formulated in one day or one month. But rather came from often spirited and acrimonious debate during the years following the end of open hostilities with the English King. But as is always the case when mortal man determines to set one canon of conditions or a single agreement on a future action, there is no easy path to immediate resolution. More often than not, consensus is born of constraint.

To many, the United States Constitution in its current form is considered the law of the land, inviolable and immune to the immediate changes so often demanded by more dissident elements. To others, it is an archaic pronouncement of individuals whose time and understanding of changing human values and societal qualifications, has long passed. Yet, to an even larger part of our population, the document remains hidden behind the veil of misunderstanding and lack of thoughtful review and more tragically, the lack of substantive education in our schools. Sadly, as important and critical to every new citizen and those reaching voting age, it is a subject miserably taught in schools or the preparatory role to citizenship for any new entry.

It is said a constitution is the act of a people to create the structure of a government. Regardless of form, a constitution should include four primary purposes; to provide the actual configuration of the governing entity. Next, it must give authority to the powers that government possesses and apportion those powers among the various branches. Third, it should stipulate those limits on the government itself. It is these stated limitations that creates the balance desired by the people. Finally, it needs to provide the reasonable system by which changes can be made in the future to rectify or clarify as need might dictate.

Since Americans have long accepted but still harbor a natural resentment against any governing authority, it must be remembered that the early founders of this country were strongly distrustful of government, born of their earlier domination by their English masters three thousand miles away. It was incumbent on the Founding Fathers to clearly enumerate what powers selected administrators had or could exercise. It is in this context that the original format for personal liberties and expression of individual rights became the dominant theme of the Declaration of Independence, the initial acts of confederation and finally the United States Constitution. It could be easily said that much of our laws were written for a different time and different conditions, long shrouded in a veil of shortened memory. However, we must be ever cognizant that as mankind has developed newer and more adventuresome soirée's into formerly undiscovered vistas of human thought and achievement, the past can still remain a beneficial guide to the future.

The law is not a benevolent master, nor is it to dictate or assess latitudes of variance allowed in its administration. That power has been entrusted in our Constitution to the courts who are supposed to be the extension of human thought, and subject to its frailties and inevitable bias. To assume exactness and correctness in its administration is to consider each snowflake a copy of its predecessor. As often as its presentation has been argued before the High Court and adjudicated, it may still seem to the casual observer as a vehicle, subject to interpretation, deviation and sadly at times, obfuscation. So let us begin the trek to dig deeper into the actual wordage of the Constitution. Not a cursory scan and not a rehashing of the supposedly wise reminisces of avowed pundits.

In prefacing any dialogue regarding this primary subject we need to clarify the word: law. The law defines boundaries and limitations to human conduct and the rights of access by the individual. Without such definition, we become a rudderless society, destined to wander aimlessly through our own lack of direction. Where there is conflict of interpretation or issues in doubt due to semantic confusion, it must first be determined if there is textually demonstrable constitutional commitment to assure the correct construction of the original and sustaining intent of the wordage in question.

There exists two differing schools of thought regarding the use of the Constitution. To the markedly conservative it is the rock on which our present form of government and all its inherent and attributed liberties rests. Never changing, it is to be immutable in its meaning. To its defenders, it is an escutcheon, borne high by those who distrust change and anyone proposing same. It has been said that the men who made the Constitution were of the mutual opinion that government was a "necessary evil." Thus they insisted that the powers ascribed to this new government be specifically stipulated. And that the Supreme Court would be the best arbiter and interpreter of that document and its eventual codes and statutes. Regrettably their well-meaning intent never fully reached fruition. To the obverse, the more liberal element feels the document should be open to constant change as desired or demanded by the current power structure and social environment.

We have long heard that government should not be an overlord of the people but rather its servant. Sadly, the opposing more liberally interpretive viewpoint considers the Constitution merely a set of rules and conditions, developed by those for whom the ages have proven were at best naïve in the changes that would evolve. To these advocates of continual political abuse, the Constitution was a menu of social conduct and conditions that would serve the populace best if constantly under review and change, where public interest is a matter of political power than personal advantage. Some feel the Constitution is not what it says but what those controlling the mantle of national administration wish to see altered to fit current public opinion or majority intent.

In this essay, we are going to look closely at the considered "Law of the Land" through the writer's eyes. It will undoubtedly be filtered by ones human nature and most assuredly a degree of bias that influences all to a varying degree. I've become far more attuned to the subject matter than I'd ever imagined when I began this strong interest almost sixty years ago. Many, whose work I've pursued and read have my deepest respect for their standing in the legal community and their evident credibility. Regrettably there are too many others who feel the Constitution is merely a casual compilation of thoughts, written to be thoroughly revised as the will of the mob or the political ambition of another of the `one world' political puppets. It is from this perch on the fence line of common sense that I pursue the ever elusive truth of fact. The Constitution sets ground rules for the allocation of authority between the two operative elements, the Executive and the Legislative. The third leg to this triangle of governmental form is the Judiciary. Their task is to ostensibly assure there will not be any exaggerated emphasis by one side or the other in the function of governing

Was the original language of the Constitution born of traditional ideologies? Of course, as these are the progenitors of all thoughts and commentary committed to the written word. Such range of consideration can shift from the idealistic to the utopian wherein all manner of evil or injustice is diminished or potentially eliminated totally. To the more astute, ideology refers to intellectual concepts. But to the realist and pragmatist, it is the substance of an individual or group's structured beliefs, religious, political or social. Unlike the disciplined thesis or dogma purported by a religion as the exact word of God, the Constitution is not a string of words in perfect order. It is flawed regardless of the sincerity of the writers' intent. So as any written document can be edited, it is subject to change. But we must be very careful that change be a limited and highly structured process. Today, the word change appears in a doctrinal sense, a contended method to achieve the betterment of the wording's intent. Those who would constantly use this verbiage intend not on improvement but as a solidification of power. And it is this ongoing struggle for power that embodies most efforts to change the United States Constitution.

The original Constitution and its accompanying additions do not form a précis. Rather, it encompasses what the writers felt were primary needs in order to accomplish their mission. It was a mission that included freedom from monarchial control and the limitations on personal rights that had enslaved mankind since the beginning of time. To others, it is a document, well-meaning in its inception but constantly in need of revision, clarification and at times immediate and measurable change in direction, however subtle or overt. A symbol of our national structure, but like the tree of liberty it has been likened to in past prose, subject to the winds of change, able to bend with the needs of societal evolution. In both camps, the fire of their zeal is so often dampened when one merely advises them that change is acceptable – in a manner prescribed by law. Amendments can and have been proffered, submitted for legislative debate and vote by that body. If successful, it is then submitted to the states for ratification, requiring thirty seven of the current fifty states to agree, thus instituting the change or revision as detailed in the offered amendment. The inevitable question is what need or proprietary authorship should generate such change. Who or what group or what ideology shall be the generator of any move or demand to create whatever change is considered in imminent need so as to assuage a misdeed or attend to a deficiency in personal liberty? That decision must lie in the hands of the citizen constituency and not at the whim or personal agenda of those who have gained elected or appointed power whether nationally or locally. The critics who feel the Constitution is totally outdated and comprised of inappropriate beliefs and dogma, must remember two very simple elements to the document's genesis. First, the Constitution is a veritable stew concocted of varied and often diverse ingredients. Its components reflected the views, opinions, the cultural ideology and unfortunately also the prejudices of the time.

For students wishing to learn more about how and in what context the original Constitution was drafted, pursuing a study of that time and thought can help – to a limited degree. It was an era when the control of the mighty was preeminent and the role of those without power was to be forever subordinate. It was a document, ennobled by the good intentions and the desire to rectify past grievances. Slavery, women's rights, voting age, the abolishing of the ignorance expressed in the prohibition amendment, all needed and received their time to be restated properly.

So now, on to the Constitution as it currently resides as the governing document of our nation. The reader will note that certain comments will tend to repeat themselves in varying manners. That is because there are similar concerns or issues pertinent to several or more Articles or Amendments. Regardless of how they might seem unconnected, they are in the light of modern review, actually related to one another, although sometimes in vague association. I've learned to minimize my dislike of the liberal elitism that resounds in many academic and politically correct articles appearing in a highly suspect media.

For the truly adventuresome in past commentary on the Constitution, I would suggest reviewing some of the rulings issued by or at times dissented with by members of the U.S. Supreme Court. There were Associate Justices Hugo Black, William O. Douglas, Benjamin Cardozo, John Marshall, William Brennan, the venerable Oliver Wendell Holmes and the much discussed Warren Burger court when he was Chief Justice. In their words lies the interpretive matrix of their particular time. And as you would soon realize, those interpretations were subject to marked change as the societal need and the inevitable motion of time occurred. At certain places, specific case law will be referred to, not to state these as some kind of deep legal treatises, but as trail markers; legal decisions that more clearly explain how subsequent language was developed based on an Amendment declaring such need. The following is meant to create discussion and thought. Realistically it is not the right of the individual to interpret the Constitution as he or she may wish and then act on that interpretation in undertaking or claiming or denying any aspect of that document. It remains the mandate of the judicial system to make such determinations.

We will in turn review these questions and comments about the Constitution relative to its current status, and a cleansing of the misinterpretations and inconsistencies articulated by both its proponents and opponents. What concerns me the most is how original concept of the Constitution and future laws created by a totally politically obsessed Congressional process, will be compatible to that same Constitution written so many years ago. Or worse yet, as eventually approved by a Supreme Court that may become an ultra-liberal bastion of thought if and when such excessively altruistic oriented future members are nominated by a White House occupant exhibiting a far more socialist bent. Many have long acknowledged the Constitution as the guiding document for our government to operate. Yet our modern political philosophy appears to lean ever more toward the provision of life services under governmental mandate and not through change of the will of the citizenry as a whole. But perhaps Thomas Jefferson said it best when he cautioned, "A government big enough to give you everything you want is strong enough to take away everything you have."

If we consider the Constitution a doctrine of laws we must further believe that the law is that cohesive substance so needed to bind ever tenuously this fragile fabric of our society. Forbearance with those who would subjugate the basic structure of the Constitution to further their own ideology is admirable. But the ultra-left and those demanding that this document become their personal template for whatever change is being pursued by public pressure or insistence by social zealots, must not be allowed to prostitute the process for orderly change as required by law.

The language of the original form of the Articles has been repeated in this writing exactly as they appear in a reproduction of the original document. So those obsessed with grammatical or punctuation revisions need to remember, what they are viewing is how the original wordage was framed and punctuated. To the politically correct, those who insist on purifying by omitting now considered unacceptable words, it is an argument bearing little relevance to this dissertation. The growing intent to cleanse the original wording of many pieces of great literature through applying the astringent of petty politicizing, is an affront to the purpose of the written word. Words are the road signs that lead us through the thoughts of the writer. Words are the monuments of man's history, indestructible regardless of the ravages of the jaded literati or the politically inculcated.

It must be recognized by the reader that per Supreme Court Justice William Randolph Hearst in a 1918 comment, "A word is not a crystal, transparent and unchanged, it is the skin of a living thought and may vary greatly in color and content according to the circumstances and the time in which it is used."

Remember, it was written by a minority of individuals with the education and proclivity to an extended use of the English language. Inasmuch as a majority of then future citizens could read very little or had limited advantage to, other than the merest scrabble of education. The Constitution and its preceding Declaration of Independence sprang from those who could and desired to provide in writing for those in need of such rights. It must also not be forgotten, the principal piece of literature and the premier published work at that time, was in fact the Holy Bible. Regardless of the many offerings of the Greek classics and myriad of other philosophers and polemicists, it still does not dampen or lessen the intent and impact of the original constitutional design other than the sophistry so common among the self-endowed savants of modern media and academia.

Regrettably, any elected President or Congressional leadership who demands social change without any voice of the people to caution or remand or secession, threatens the solidarity of the document's original intent. Thus the need to again, in the opinion of the author, revise his earlier productions of this treatise. It is not a close reading of the Constitution or excessive scrutiny that is required, but rather recognition that to effect those changes desired by the reigning power structure, the simple procedure reflected in the Constitution dictates public presentation and eventual acceptance of any such changes through a citizen vote. Only then will change occur in a legal, moral and ethical manner.

Regardless, whether the reader desires to limit the increasing reach of the government or feels this document should encompass the total needs of the constituency without question concerning requested entitlement or granted emoluments, it is an instrument unique in the recorded history of mankind. It stands as a symbol of individual freedom, never before proposed and implemented however criticized, interpreted or possibly needing review it has been over the past 230 years.

● ● ●

The Constitution of the United States of America

Article I

SECTION 1 - All legislative Powers herein granted shall be vested in a congress of the United States, which shall consist of a Senate and House of Representatives.

COMMENT: This is the statutory constitutional requirement that only the legislature should create and forward laws, determining policies and all effective rules for operation of the government and its administration for the benefit and betterment of the public constituency. Here is where the Constitutional rubber must hit the mandated road, as it were. As will be later argued, it has been more common over the past several decades for the judiciary at all levels to seek to set social policy. Bluntly stated, that is not their responsibility or their rightful position as the Constitution currently exists. This we shall pursue when that body's enumeration of rights is further detailed. Until reconstituted or invigorated by a new found sense of obligation to the people's primary needs, this body, as will the Senate, continue to debate their personal agendas in conflict with that of their constituencies. It is this phrase "... all legislative powers shall... be vested in a Congress" that has supported many claims to reduce the Supreme Court's ability to alter or diminish the power of any law through review and adjudication.

This writer cannot project or propose any potential answer for alleviating the current quandary faced in the public opinion as to the ongoing inability of the two bodies or their respective political entities to achieve a modicum of agreement, compromise, or mutual understanding of the many issues facing the legislative process.

SECTION 2 – The House of Representatives shall be composed of members chosen every second year by the people of the several States and the Electors in each State shall have the qualifications requisite for Electors of the most numerous Branch of the State legislature.

COMMENT: Regardless of the seeming semantic convolution, the basic premise insures direct election of those who would speak for the people they represent. It is this writer's opinion, however, that possibly a part of the ongoing stagnation that occurs even when electoral changes occur in the Congress or Executive Branch, involves the apparent unrelenting need for each representative to pursue reelection. With one short year under their belt, House of Representative members are then vigorously on the campaign trail to hopefully be given the votes to return to the Halls of Congress the next year. Were that two year term extended to three years, would not a greater balance and stability be accomplished? A more solid representation could be achieved. A sense of maturity of legislative input might lessen this hurried race to seek support at the ballot box while attempting to assure that which most benefits both individual constituency and the country as a whole?

SECTION 2 [continued] No person shall be a representative who shall not have attained to the age of 25 years, and been seven years a Citizen of the United States, and who shall not, when elected, be an inhabitant of that State in which he shall be chosen. [Representatives and direct taxes shall be apportioned among the several states which may be included within this Union according to their respective numbers. Which shall be determined by adding to the whole number of free persons, including those bound to service for a term of years and *excluding Indians not taxed, three-fifths of all other persons.] **

The actual enumeration shall be made within three years after the first meeting of the Congress of the United States, and within every subsequent term of 10 years, in such manner as they shall by law, direct. The number of Representatives shall not exceed one for every 30,000, but each state shall have at least one representative; and until such enumeration shall be made, the State of New Hampshire shall be entitled to call chuse three, Massachusetts eight, Rhode Island and Providence plantations one, Connecticut five, New York six, New Jersey four, Pennsylvania eight, Delaware one, Maryland six, Virginia ten, North Carolina five, South Carolina five and Georgia three.

When vacancies happen in the representation from any State the executive authority thereof shall issue writs of election to fill such vacancies. The House of Representatives shall choose their Speaker and other officers; and shall have the sole power of impeachment.

SECTION 3. The Senate of the United States shall be composed of two Senators from each state, chosen by the Legislature thereof, for six years; and each Sen. shall have one vote. Immediately after they shall be assembled in consequence of the first election, and if vacancies happen by resignation, or otherwise, during the recess of the Legislature of any state, the executive thereof may make temporary appointments until the next meeting of the Legislature, which shall then fill such vacancies.

COMMENT: And it is this opportunity to appoint those to fill vacancies in either house that too often creates the political chicanery within local elective influence. In a number of states, such appointment privilege is tantamount to a lottery of favors as to what can be gained by either the appointer or the administration in power. Without a required selection process controlled by the right of vote by the citizenry, we continue to be bound by rulers in which we have no voice or have lost confidence to hear the voice or the constituency.

There has arisen the question of "natural born citizenship" referring to presidential and vice presidential candidates. Until resolved as to any change in the "birth" requirement now in effect, the problem of accession remains a problem as those in the chain of succession would be ineligible were any situation require reaching into the list of stipulated congressional leadership or cabinet officers if not "naturally born citizens" as currently prescribed.

Were state administrations required in every instance to allow the pertinent constituency to vote on any such replacement for the congressional position vacated by death, inability to perform or other reasons, several exceptions could be plausible alternatives. If the next election for that particular position is less than six months in the future or the replacement is merely a place holder until other candidates can be offered to the constituency for a vote.

(Section 3, continued.) No Person shall be a Senator who shall not have attained to the age of 30 years and been nine years a Citizen of the United States, and who shall not when elected, be an inhabitant of that State for which he shall be chosen.

COMMENT: This requirement has become one of the most implausible aspects of the residency clause. The phraseology in itself is rather obfuscated and may need a close and definitive review. As an example, a recent presidential candidate had earlier in her congressional bid, merely purchased a home in the state of desired Senatorial position. She then blatantly declared herself a resident of that state without any conscious length of residency there. Seeking advantage to the lack of concern for the constituency in the desired area is more a matter of personal hypocrisy than value to the voter. As to the Presidency, that issue as to eligibility was defined in Section 1, Article II, covered later in this dissertation and as regards the required "natural born Citizen" categorization.

The question of natural born citizenry reached its most public and rancorous dialogue with the election of the first black individual in 2008. The individual's actual birthplace was held in doubt by his critics and opponents for many months. The question, was he actually born in Hawaii, a state in the union or possibly the home country of his biological father, the country of Kenya. That and his somewhat circuitous travels from childhood to his final destination in the United States created a controversy that threatened to invalidate his election if ever proven he was not native born. Because of the delay in producing documentation verifying his birth as an American citizen, the newly elected president appeared to ignore this growing concern. Eventually the sufficient documentation was provided. The question remains. Why such a delay when ones genealogy is something of which to be proud unless not definitive by fact? He could have easily produced the valid birth certificate early during the inquiry and the entire matter would have as quickly vanished from public thought or media concern. His claim and that of his supporters that such documentation was not required or mandated merely furthered the exaggerated media tumult.

Yet there has long been the argument of what the term "natural born citizen" actually defines as to eligibility. Some would have that phrase changed to only a legitimate or verified citizenship but long ago countered by the Alexander Hamilton insistence it would preclude foreign influence through a non-citizen attaining the office. Since the term "natural born" citizen is not defined in the Constitution and there appears no commentary in the Federal convention of 1787 it has been suggested the term may have been merely suggested in a letter from John Jay to George Washington. Jay, who would become the first Chief Justice of the Supreme Court in 1789, staying on the bench until 1795, expressed the need that the position of "Commander-in-chief be nothing less than a natural born citizen."

However, the discussion will undoubtedly continue for years to come unless constitutionally clarified through change. To reduce any future controversy as to the question of legitimacy to the Office of the President, I would propose that all contenders for that office, including that of the Vice Presidency and Speaker of the House of Representatives (second in line were the President to be deceased or unable to perform the duties of that office), be required, if challenged to present verifiable documentation of their native citizenship as mandated in the Constitution. And this stipulation should remain unless and until such prerequisite be changed by appropriate amendment to the Constitution.

(Section 3, continued.) The Vice President of the United States shall be President of the Senate, but shall have no vote, unless they be equally divided. The Senate shall choose their other officers, and also a President Pro tempore, in the absence of the Vice President, or when he shall exercise the office of President of the United States. The Senate shall have sole power to try all impeachments. When sitting for that purpose they shall be on oath or affirmation. When the President of the United States is tried, the Chief Justice shall provide: and no person shall be convicted without concurrence of two thirds of the members present.

COMMENT: Without any defined powers other than as abstractly described, the Vice President too often spends his days fulfilling the myriad of public functions either not on the President's schedule or considered too mundane or politically ineffective. There is a humorous commentary on this unique position; "A woman had two sons, one went to sea and the other becoming Vice President of the United States. Neither was ever heard of again." One of TV's better known comics once noted, "The major task a Vice President undertakes is to check the obituary page each morning to see if he has another job." We have been fortunate over the years to have had a few strong and eventually proven very able successors to the Presidency when death removed the incumbent. Regrettably that has not always been the case. Too often the Vice

Presidential slot on the national election ticket is used to fulfill campaign promises or pacify an important and potentially divisive segment of the principal candidate's party.

(Section 3, continued.) Judgment in cases of impeachment shall not extend further than to removal from office, and disqualification to hold and enjoy any office of honor, trust, or profit under the United States. But the party convicted shall nevertheless be liable and subject to indictment, trial judgment and punishment, according to the law at the time of the accused offense.

COMMENT: A question arises as to whether a citizen based legal action or action brought by any particular group can be submitted against any impeached official. This would include assurance that all previously mandated or due pensions or other such benefits be removed and no longer enjoyed at a cost to the tax paying public. Again, the continuing argument for and against term limits for both houses raises the concept of a greater involvement by members of a society, too often denied a voice due to the extended tenure of those previously elected. Thus, were the senatorial terms reduced to five years, many elections for both houses would occur in off years from the quadrennial presidential bid. This might provide access by many more potential candidates, not being tied to those periodic attempts by one party or the other to totally change the control of power in Washington. This writer is a confirmed advocate for term limits for all congressional positions as shall be referred to in later passages. We have developed a career path never intended by our founding Fathers. One that has further created the phlegmatic nature of our legislative process.

SECTION 4. The times and places, and manner of holding elections for Senators and Representatives, shall be prescribed in each State by the Legislature thereof; but the Congress may at any time by law make or alter such regulations, except as to the places of choosing Senators the Congress, shall assemble at least once in every year and such meetings shall be on the first Monday in December unless they shall by law appoint a different day.

COMMENT: Here we have the direct conflict between the rights of the states and the contended interference by the federal government into the ability of each state to control the elective process. The current US Attorney General at this writing, has taken a forceful stand against several states that require a photo identification form to validate a voter. Although a mélange of required photo ID's currently exists in order to acquire or achieve access to or provision of documentation, here is where the "states right" aspect comes to the fore. If the national administration can control that element of voter process, it becomes a controlling factor totally in opposition to the intent of the Founding Fathers. So long as the individual state voting requirements do not refer to or limit access by race, sex, religion or other defining personal qualifications, it should be the state's right to assure a method to minimize voter fraud.

The current Administration contends that many Latinos and others of minority categories, have no such photo application such as would exist with a valid driver's license. The question continues, what creates eligibility for a photo identification that would allow the holder to vote – citizenship? If that is not required, then the appropriate amendment should be developed and required that the mandatory number of states approve such a change. Sadly, such an occurrence would mark the end of the totality and protection of all legitimate citizens.

To demand acquiring such an ID through the state is argued as the creation of a national ID to be carried by every individual in this country. This is an anathema to the more liberal causes but considered by others as necessary protection of the citizen which choruses the more conservative viewpoint. Still, it appears the only action of import not requiring photo identification of some nature seems to be voting. One of the most sacred and valued freedoms we as a society enjoy and one of the nationally proscribed processes most vulnerable to fraud or deceit. The primaries in each state have become quagmires of differing political philosophies and rank discord among those seeking to use these preliminaries to either secure their position or best their opponent. The constant race to be the first primary on a national scale has turned the process into a veritable circus of juvenile pique and questionable behavior on both local and state level. We are required a plethora of identification at airports, seeking travel documents, visas, passports, bank transactions seeking financial assistance, the list is seemingly unending. Can we not require similar safeguards for the most important right any citizen has – to vote?

SECTION 5. Each house shall be the judge of the elections, returns and qualifications of its own members, and a majority of each shall constitute a quorum to do business; but a smaller number may adjourn from day to day and may be authorized to compel the attendance of absent members, in such manner, and under such penalties as each House may provide. Each House may determine the rules of its proceedings, punish its members for disorderly behavior, and with the concurrence of two thirds, expel a member. Each House shall keep a Journal of its proceedings, and from time to time publish the same, excepting such parts as may in their judgment require secrecy; and the yeas and nays of the members of each House on any question shall, at the desire of one fifth of those present, be entered on the Journal. Neither House, during the session of Congress, shall without the consent of the other, or just adjourn for more than three days, nor to any other Place than that in which the two houses shall be sitting.

COMMENT: Here again we find our legislative process being continually mired in a desire of legislators to spend as little time possible at their assigned tasks. Or more possibly, to use the taxpayer's financial support to use valuable deliberative time to merely posture in an attempt to assure future voting majorities during the next election campaign.

Regrettably, this constitutional provision regarding the sitting of either legislative body, has become ample fodder for a sitting Chief Executive to appoint and designate while bypassing legislative approval. This writer suggests:

"That Congress shall publish no less than ten days prior to the beginning of each mandated session, those days of each week when the congress reasonably expects and has planned to be in session and available to conduct the business of the people. Furthermore, that when legislation is required to complete or extend in the interest of the people, processes, including but not limited to passage of a budget, completion of hearings related to Presidential and Judicial appointments, unless a majority vote is held and so recorded delaying such actions, the elected representatives shall continue and strive to complete such actions as referred to herein. Additionally, vacation or extended adjournments within each session shall be so noted and publicized in advance so as to inform the general populace when such absence from their mandated functions will occur."

SECTION 6. The Senators and Representatives shall receive a compensation for their services, to be ascertained by law and paid out of the treasury of the United States they shall in all cases, except treason, felony, and breach of the peace, be privileged from arrest during their attendance at the session of their respective houses, and in going to and returning from the same.; and for any speech or debate in either House, they shall not be questioned in any other place.

No senator or representative shall, during the time for which he was elected, be appointed to any civil office under the authority of the United States, which shall have been created, or the emoluments whereof shall have been encreased during such time; and no person holding any office under the United States, shall be a member of either house during

his continuance in office.

SECTION 7. All bills for raising revenue shall originate in the House of Representatives; but the Senate may propose or concur with amendments as on other bills.

Every Bill which shall have passed the House of Representatives and the Senate, shall, before it become a Law, be presented to the President of the United States; if he approve he shall sign it, but if not he shall return it, with his objections to that House in which it shall have originated, who shall enter the objections at large on their Journal, and proceed to reconsider it. If after such reconsideration two thirds of that House shall agree to pass the Bill, it shall be sent together with the objections, to the other House, by which it shall likewise be reconsidered, and if approved by two thirds of that House, it shall become a law. But in all such cases the votes of both houses shall be determined by yeas and nays, and the names of the persons voting for and against the Bill shall be entered on the Journal of each House respectively. If any Bill shall not be returned by the Pres. within 10 days parentheses Sundays excepted) after it shall have been presented to him, the same shall be a Law, in like manner as if he had signed it, unless the Congress by their adjournment prevent its return in which case it shall not be a law.

Every order, resolution, or vote to which the concurrence of the Senate and House of Representatives may be necessary parentheses except on a question of adjournment parentheses shall be presented to the President of the United States; and, before the same shall take effect, shall be approved by him, or being disapproved by him, shall be repassed by two-thirds of the Senate and House of Representatives,

according to the rules and limitations prescribed in the case of a Bill.

COMMENT: A major complaint by many citizen groups direct criticism at the apparent laxity of both Houses of Congress to spend sufficient time developing, discussing and either passing or negating legislation. There are the excessive periods of non-activity, extended vacations and the inevitable shortened period of deliberation each week caused by the constant travel back and forth between Washington and the individual solon's home base. This seeming excess expenditure at tax payer expense has long become a thorn in the side of the citizenry who themselves, find even the simplest necessities a strain on their personal budget. Please note this writer's suggestion as was proffered in reference to Section 5 of this article.

Another disturbing allowance within this section, directly provides all members of Congress a right precluded by law for every other citizen. That of protection from libel and slander laws so long as their comments are made from the floor of that establishment. Such protection has also been carried further into the so-called official committee hearings held in the Capitol building. This immunity allows a member to decry, proclaim, declare, state without reservation, complaint, contended misdeed by others (nonmembers of that body) even though such remarks as spoken and/or made part of the official Congressional Record are found to be without substance, factual support or proven validity. Others, not provided this immunity, could and would often be accused and at times prosecuted for the same unsupported dalliance with the truth. Justice Joseph Story, (1779-1845) of the USSCT, noted for his opinion shaping Commentaries of the US constitution (1833) regarding the part of the section reference, ". . . that for any speech or debate in either, they shall not be questioned in any other place," he wrote; "No man ought to have a right to defame others under the color of a performance of the duties of his office."

This abuse of the protection against such derogatory dialogue by an elected member of congress is an affront to the original purpose of those laws concerning purposeful or harmful denigration or vilification from the floor of either house. The Court has ruled on a number of occasions that such immunity continues whether forwarding or continuing any such statements in media releases, speeches or interviews outside the protective cloak of Congress. The arrest prohibition should remain but there should be a direct reference to any verbal onslaughts by members of either house. This writer would suggest the appropriate development of caution within this section by amending the language as follows.

"That declarations, statements, contentions and directed conclusions made by any member outside the legislative body of either House, be subject to any and all recourse that might be taken by an aggrieved citizen who can present a palpable charge of damage to good name, reputation or economic disadvantage. And that such charge be issued forthwith and be allowed suitable processing within the jurisdiction available at the time. And that said member of either house may be challenged by any recipient of such statements or comments uttered during the protected ambience and required to add to or substantiate such protected commentary if a charge of defamation, damage to reputation or economic disadvantage should be proved by such recipient."

SECTION 8. The Congress shall have power to lay and collect taxes or duties imposed and exercises to pay the debts and provide for the common defense and general welfare of the United States; but all duties, imposed and exercises shall be uniform throughout the United States; To borrow Money on the credit of the United States, To regulate commerce with foreign Nations, and among the several states and with the Indian tribes; To establish an uniform rule of naturalization and uniform laws on the subject of bankruptcies throughout the United States; To coin money, regulate the value thereof, and of foreign coin's and fix the standard of weights and measures; to provide for the punishment of counterfeiting the securities and current coin of the United States; To establish post offices and post Roads; To promote the

progress of science and useful arts by securing for limited times to authors and inventors the exclusive right to their respective writings and discoveries to constitute tribunals inferior to the Supreme Court; To define and publish punish piracies and felonies committed on the high seas, and offenses against the law of nations; to declare war grant letters of Mark and reprisal and make rules concerning captures on land and water to raise and support armies, but no appropriation of Money to that use shall be for a longer term than two years to provide and maintain a Navy; To make rules for the government and regulation of the land and naval forces; To provide for calling forth the militia to execute the laws of the Union, suppress insurrections and repel invasions;

To provide for organizing, arming, and disciplining the militia, and for governing such part of them as may be employed in the service of the United States, reserving to the states respectively, the appointment of the officers and Authority of training the militia according to the discipline prescribed by Congress;

To exercise exclusive legislation in all cases whatsoever, over such District (not exceeding ten miles square) as may, by cession of particular states, and the acceptance of Congress, become the seat of the government of the United States), and to exercise like Authority over all places purchased by the consent of the legislature of the state in which the same shall be for the erection of forts, magazines, arsenals, dock-yards, and other needful buildings; - And

To make all laws to which shall be necessary and proper for carrying into execution the foregoing powers, and all other Powers vested by this Constitution in the Government of the United States, or in any department or officer thereof.

COMMENT: Section 8 also directs the government to establish a uniform rule of naturalization. Apparently either disregarded or desirous of supplementing with the series of recent Executive orders granting permanent occupancy in the country for millions of heretofore illegal or "undocumented" individuals. It is within this section that the current explosion of public disagreement and litigation brought by twenty six states has occurred. If this dissertation ever sees public print or wider distribution, this matter was ostensibly resolved in the "Patient Protection and Affordable Care Act" legal action litigated before the High court. More commonly referred to as the "Obamacare case", it challenged the intent and purpose of the "commerce clause." As to whether Congress or the Executive Department can in fact dictate actions of their constituency is not clearly identified in the rights and limitations of power as expressly demonstrated within the Constitution; an issue that still has not been successfully resolved. The plaintiffs have claimed that judicial acceptance of the declared right of the Administration to control required health care with potential penalty or "tax" as some contend, will, in fact give the Executive Branch continuing power to require other conditions of employment, use and distribution heretofore prohibited by that same Congress.

With the massive migration of illegal entrants and the apparent disregard of the national administration to enact measures to assure a lessening of this problem, another even more disconcerting movement has become evident. Basically referred to as "sanctuary cities", these urban centers whose local administration, often including their police segment, refuse to notify the Immigration and Customs Enforcement department when an individual, accused and/or convicted of illegal offenses and with no proof of legal presence in this country are in their custody. This blatant act, although seemingly smothered in avowed desires to be humane and sensitive to the undocumented, is in total and absolute violation of both the Constitution and the Letter of the Law which is the inherent responsibility of every jurisdiction. Without this needed connection and cooperation, the flood of many who may be a danger and threat to others within the communities are being allowed to reside due to the absence of appropriate legal restraint. It is a matter the incoming administration as a result of the 2016 national election will have to confront.

Harkening back to Marbury v. Madison, 5 U.S. (1 Cranch 137) 1803, this particular case has been consistently stated by the Court that it "emphatically declares the province and duty of the judiciary to determine the constitutionality of a statute or created or enacted law." It is this self-espoused mandate that continues the High Court's continual intervening in legislative matters over the past century. Another instance where the court did agree with the Administration's claim to control a subject within this clause would be United States vs. Butler, 297 U.S. 1 (1936) a matter regarding the Agricultural Act of 1933. In which it was adjudicated that a tax could be assessed on farmers to control overly expanded crop production that would affix prices to the detriment of the consumer. This became a hallmark instance related to the often contested "general welfare" right of the federal government.

Supporters of the present insistence that government has a greater right to intervene in this "general welfare" concept would be the Lochner vs. New York, 198 U.S. 45(1905). In this instance, the Supreme Court ruled that a New York law limiting the number of hours a baker could work each week to sixty hours was a labor law attempting to regulate terms of employment. Thus, holding that the "liberty of contract" was an implicit right and not to be altered or shaped by the federal government. The concern many have, is a growing opinion that if the act is found constitutional by the High Court and the law stands as earlier mandated, it will indicate the current Administration's determined move toward a more socialist oriented government. That if approved, this format of governmental oversight will allow demands on the citizenry formerly thought out of the purview of national authorities. That it will also further impinge on the rights of states as are enumerated in both this clause and other portions of the Constitution.

SECTION 9 The migration or importation of such persons as any states now existing shall think proper to admit, shall not be prohibited

by the Congress prior to the year 1808, but a tax or duty may be imposed on such importation, not exceeding $10 for each person. The privilege of the writ of habeas corpus shall not be suspended, unless when in cases of rebellion or invasion the public safety may require it no Bill of attainder or ex post facto law shall be passed no capitalization or other direct tax, shall be laid unless in proportion to the senses or enumeration herein before directed to be taken. No tax or duty shall be laid on articles exported from any State. No preference shall be given by any regulation of commerce or revenue to the ports of one State over those of another: nor shall vessels bound to, or from one State, be obliged to enter, clear, or pay duties in another paragraph no money shall be drawn from the treasury, but in consequence of appropriations made by Law; and a regular statement and account of the receipts and expenditures of all public Money shall be published from time to time. No title of nobility shall be granted by the United States and no person holding any office or of profit or trust under them shall, without the consent of Congress, except in the present him only month office, or title, of any kind whatever from any King, Prince or foreign state.

COMMENT: A critical condition in this section, too often overlooked when teaching the constitutional basics is the prohibition against abeyance of suspension of the Writ of Habeas Corpus, the ultimate legal protection for individuals. Only in incidences of insurrection or as stated in the original document, rebellion or invasion. Although history reflects its controversial use several times in the past, it remains the hallmark of personal freedom from illegal or improper incursion onto the person, dwelling and property. This can assure no individual is taken and held incommunicado, a process so common in many other countries. Eliminating the depriving one of their liberty without legal and proper process is the definitive quantification of what early Americans demanded.

SECTION 10. No State shall enter into any treaty alliance, or

Confederation; grant letters of Marque and reprisal; coin Money; emit bills of credit; make anything but gold and silver coin a tender in payment of debts; pass any Bill of attainder ex post facto law, or law impairing the obligation of contracts, or grant any title of nobility. Paragraph no state shall without the consent of Congress lay any imposts or duties on imports or exports, except that which may be absolutely necessary for executing it's inspection laws: and the net produce of all duties and impose, laid by any State on imports or exports, shall be for the use of the treasury of the United States; and all such laws shall be subject to the revision and control of the Congress paragraph no state shall with, without the consent of Congress lay any duty of tonnage keep troops or ships of war in time of peace, enter into any agreement or compact with another State, or with a foreign power, or engage in war, unless actually invaded, or in such imminent danger as will not admit of delay.

COMMENT: Within this clause lie numerous issues creating ongoing conflict between the state and the national administration. Primarily it reflects the interest and desire of either to control their own operational dominance in many aspects of economic, social and political venues. Thus the ever present "states' rights" dispute became a principal point of controversy and argument among the original writers of the Constitution. The differences between the diverse cultures of each of the colonies caused constant demand by the smaller colonies and less advantaged members that each colony – state – retain their individual freedom to machinate their particular area without possible monarchial interference by any central government. Too often overlooked when teaching the constitutional basics to students, is the prohibition against abeyance or suspension of the writ of habeas corpus. Its proper use entails legal and appropriately mandated imprisonment.

● ● ●

● ● ●

ARTICLE II

The executive power shall be vested in a President of the United States of America. He shall hold his office during the term of four years and together with the vice-president, chosen for the same term, be elected as, as follows. Each state shall appoint, in such manner as the Legislature thereof may direct, a number of electors equal to the whole number of Senators and Representatives to which the State may be entitled in the Congress: but no senator or representative, or person holding an office of trust or profit under the United States, shall be appointed an elector.

The electors shall meet in their respective states and vote by ballot for two persons, of whom one at least shall not be an inhabitant of the same state with themselves and they shall make a list of all the persons voted for, and of the number of votes for each; which list they shall sign and certify and transmit sealed to the seat of government of the United States, directed to the president of the Senate. The president of the Senate shall in the presence of the Senate and House of Representatives, open all the certificates and the votes shall then be counted. The person having the greatest number of votes shall be the Pres., if such number be a majority of the whole number of electors appointed; and if there be more than one who have such majority, and have an equal number of votes, then the House of Representatives shall immediately choose by ballot one of them for Pres.; and if no person have a majority, then from the five highest on the list the said House shall in like manner choose the president. But in choosing the President, the votes shall be taken by states, the representation from each state having one vote; a quorum for this person shall purpose shall consist of a member or members from two thirds of the states, and a majority of all states shall be necessary to a Choice. In every case, after the choice of the President, the person having the greatest number of votes of the electors shall be the Vice President. But if there should remain two or more who have equal votes, the Senate shall choose from them by Ballot the vice president.

[Note: this previous paragraph was changed by the 12th Amendment]

The Congress may determine the time of chusing the electors, and the day on which they shall give their votes; which day shall be the same throughout the United States.

No person except a natural born citizen, or a citizen of the United States, at the time of the adoption of this Constitution, shall be eligible to the office of President; neither shall any person be eligible to that office who shall not have attained the age of 35 years, and been 14 years a resident within the United States.

In case of the removal of the president from the office, or his death resignation, or inability to discharge the powers and duty of the said office, the same shall devolve on the VP, in the Congress made by law provide for the case of removal death resignation or inability, both of the President and Vice President, declaring what Officer shall then act as President, and such officer shall act accordingly until the disability be removed, or present shall be elected.

[Note: this preceding paragraph was affected by the 25th Amendment]

COMMENT: The Electoral College, long a bone of contention among those demanding the popular election of the President has again risen to the forefront of modern commentary by media and critics alike. The recent national election has brought forth claims of voting irregularities, never distant from any final results. Yet, challenges made by one minor national candidate and supported by the loser in the principal candidate race brings forward the need to review both proposed systems – the current Electoral College, and a pure selection by popular vote – the mathematics of who gains the most votes regardless of any other method. However, two states already utilize a "proportional" allotment of electoral votes by the percentage of popular votes gained. Would this be a satisfactory approach? The supporters of either method for determining the elected victor have always raised substantive arguments contending their version provides the truest result of each national election.

First, it is contended by supporters of the Electoral College system that it allows lesser populated states and urban areas to have a merit of reasonable influence in the final result. Were a straight popular vote to be the norm, critics dispute it is feasible that twelve or so states could so dominate the totals as to leave a majority of states and urban areas without any degree of influence in future contests. The subject will continue to be both controversial in preference and as difficult to detail as to format. To alter what is now a part of Article II of the Constitution would probably require an amendment to that same document, a process which could be fraught with claims of partisanship. However, inasmuch as each state does control the election process in their individual domain, many of their legislatures could, like Maine and Nebraska, enact proportional selection of electors. A change that might easily change the entire subject of one citizen – one vote.

One needs to stop here and reflect on the common phrase, "one man – one vote." Should we return to a system used in so many elections in our country, the majority of those voting for a measure or a candidate, succeeds in their voice being the determining factor in any issue wherein they are mandated the right to make such choices. Many have declared the electoral vote system is both stilted and often subject to machination and fraudulent application. It has been administered in various manners in every state. This entangled interpretation is the tool of the power structure, some will claim.

Others feel it has ostensibly worked sufficiently for well over two centuries, why change it now. To the lesser informed on this subject, to those wishing a speedy resolution based on their personal concept of individual right, one salient factor remains in reviewing the question of the elector system over a freewheeling selection by total popular vote: The sovereignty of the individual state, commonly referred to as state's rights, or province of the individual citizen control of the whole, still resides in the minds of each of the fifty states they must be assured the specific right to control the elective process both locally and nationally. The Founding Fathers faced this demand by each of the colonies to retain their right of individual choice and free determination in many of the aspects of self-government. And today, two hundred and forty years later that requirement has never wavered in resolve and intensity.

A concern to some is the minimizing of certain voting constituencies, the impoverished, minorities, newly admitted individuals to citizenship; the list is endless. It has been declared that to allow such a national vote purely by the eligible voter base without the process of selecting electors, would create an untenable situation for primary candidates. The proponents contend the inability to address the total eligible voting public would limit the candidate's ability to focus on certain areas and targeted groups. Critics quickly point to an ever expanding print and electronic media that provides expanding means for both attracting the attention and allowing them to respond in the increase in print forms and electronic enhancements, including television, "Twitter", "Facebook" and other such social media access. Those demanding the repeal of the Electoral College concept declare the system is outmoded, unfair to many areas of society and too subject to flaw and possible corruption.

An additional rub has occurred with the highly publicized and contested "birther" issue in which it has been claimed the former President at the time of this writing, was not in fact a native born citizen of the United States. Hopefully it is an issue that has been resolved regardless of the individual's constant denial to provide the requested documentation, until public and media pressure required him to act. This reticence was an unnecessary distraction to the proper governance of the country's interests. It provided division even among the new president's supporters by causing questions that could have easily and quickly been answered. Yet, there appears to this writer, somewhat of a conflict with the "natural born" precept and the later phrase, "and been fourteen years a resident within the United States." The two can cause discussion as to whether citizenship is an interpreted status and not specifically declared. Perhaps it is time that a rule of conduct should ensue for all those reaching the final candidacy for both the Presidency, Vice Presidency and Speaker of the House – also in line in the event the Presidency position is vacated.

"That upon obtaining nomination to the position of President and/or Vice President by his or her party, said candidates shall produce verifiable and acceptable proof of their citizenship by birth within the United States or the existing American Territories. Furthermore, such presented documentation shall be made available in a form allowing both inspection and investigation by those dissenting and who have proven standing within the judicial process for such dissent and inspection. Said review to occur and be resolved no less than sixty days prior to the election which said candidates have been nominated."

This of course could become moot should an amendment to the Constitution enable those not of native birth to become candidate for the positions as described herein. One of the more recent debates has dealt with the Presidential power to pardon. Such diminution of sentences or total legal absolutions has produced lists of individuals often considered far beyond the pale of forgiveness and return to full rights of citizenship. A previous Chief Executive utilized this power to such an egregious manner as to cast a stain of political recompense on his executive forgiveness of those duly convicted of measurable crimes. I would suggest the following addition or clarification.

"It shall be required that the President or any other executive officer holding the legal right to administer and/or institute pardons for those individuals having been previously convicted and subject to denial of rights of citizenship, be required to produce for full public view, the names, offenses and extent of incarceration if any of those individuals such Chief Executive Officer intends to dispense a pardon or other forgiveness of such past legal actions or offenses."

(Article II, continued.) The president shall, at stated times receive for his services, a compensation, which shall neither be increased or diminished during the period for which he shall have been elected, and he shall not receive within that period any other him only a month from the United States or any of them. Before he enter on execution of his office he shall take the following oath or affirmation: quote I do solemnly swear parentheses or affirm parentheses that I will faithfully execute the office is president of the United States, and will to the best of my ability, preserve, protect and defend the Constitution of the United States.

COMMENT: An interesting question has come to mind – at least in this writer's imagination, as to what could occur in the not too distant future? What if the individual stipulates that as an atheist or agnostic, he or she will not place their hand on any religious volume, be it a Torah, the Bible, the Koran or any other recognized volume of religious doctrine? Is there a requirement that said oath must be delivered as it has traditionally for over the last two hundred and thirty plus years? What if other groups demand an acceptance of the oath as an affirmation of a faith in a higher authority than the office for which the individual is being sworn? Possibly just a bit of semantic imagery; however, it could cause legal claims that the office was being installed illegally. That his or her denial of the understanding of a majority of the constituency regarding the Constitution the individual is swearing to "preserve, protect and defend," conflicts with their intent when allowing his or her receipt of the position.

It has been agreed that this nation was founded by a group of individuals who believed in, although at times varied, a general Christian code of conduct and acceptance of some form of supreme oversight. Through the many years since its inception, our nation has become a veritable polyglot of religious, social, political, economic and philosophical variations. We are the mentors of a cook's stew of often conflicting and at times fiercely defended propositions and formulae for living that fills volumes of references and the dialogue of many espousers of the arcane. What then should be the correct approach to any oath of allegiance to both the Constitution and the rule of law as it exists at the time of the oath taking? A question fraught with fervor by some but little concern by many others.

The most recent resident of the White House has been criticized as an excessively wealthy business entrepreneur or "tycoon" depending on the speaker's particular political bent. Other president has also entered that office being the owner or inheritor of rather incomes and assets. However, the nature of the inhabitant, wealth, religion, political or social ideologies has and will continue to be the meat of media grinders. Regardless of individual circumstances there may be a need for appropriate legislation to require in all such situations a predetermined time frame wherein said new incumbent place such assets in a non-voting or personally controlled trust during the term of the office. It can be part of the "transparency" so lauded by candidates during the campaign furor.

Section 2. The president shall be commander-in-chief of the Army and Navy of the United States and of the militia of the several states, when called into actual service of the United States; he may require the opinion in writing of the principal officer of each of the executive departments upon any subject relating to the duties of their respective office and he shall have power to grant reprieves and pardons for offenses against the United States, except in cases of impeachment.

He shall have power but, by and with advice and consent of the Senate, to make treaties, provided two thirds of the Senators present concur; and he shall nominate and by and with the advice and consent of the Senate, shall appoint ambassadors, other public ministers and consuls, Judges of the Supreme Court, and all other officers of the United States whose appointments are not herein otherwise provided for, and which shall be established by law school and but the Congress may by Law vest the appointment of such inferior officers, as they think proper, in the Pres. alone, in the courts of law, or in the heads of department. The president shall have the power to fill up all vacancies that may happen during the recess of the Senate, by granting commissions which shall expire at the end of their next session.

COMMENT: It is these summary appointments without legislative review, counsel or approval that has caused much consternation among opposition political hierarchy and legislators in recent years. We currently have a multiple of "czars" appointed without such process. Individuals who appear to have a degree of governing power to make decisions placed out of the range of congressional review or judicial comment.

This indistinct level of appointive power will continue to beleaguer political opponents to whomever exercises this right. The often argued right of the Executive Branch to function with expansive powers not enumerated within the Constitution was reflected in Marbury v. Madison, 5 U.S. (1 Cranch) 137, 2L, ED 60 (1803). It did not however, with its somewhat convoluted opinion, truly define the boundary between the Judiciary and Executive Branch. Wherein: President Madison's action demanding his Secretary of State to perform an action which was refused, violated the extent of his power. However, the opinion also refused constitutional acceptance of Marbury's position in the matter, leaving the question still succinctly resolved. The New Deal era of the Roosevelt presidency was most likely the best and most definitive example of growth of government. Additionally, the expansiveness of Presidential power and determined efforts to rise above the equality of the constitutionally mandated three separate branch concept.

At the time of this writing, the United States Supreme Court was hearing oral arguments, re: NLRB v. Canning. A complaint brought in contestation of the sitting President's use of the expression "recess of legislature" to appoint members of the National Labor Relations board. These nominations not submitted to Congress or for appropriate debate as to possible approval by that body. The argument of the plaintiff refers to what has been declared as a non-fact that Congress was not in legal recess. Thus the then sitting President was criticized he had sought his own ends by subverting the Constitutional requirement and claiming his definition of a congressional recess was sufficient grounds for his use of the Executive Order right granted him by the constitution.

Although the individual in that position may not have utilized that aspect of the presidency as much as a number of his predecessors, he has in the opinion of his critics wielded a rather dubious constitutional mace that has, per the opposition party relinquished public input through its legislators literally impotent. But to quantify the effect of various orders would require a closer inspection. His detractors contend that President Barack Hussein Obama had been far more demanding of change to meet his particular social agenda than any previous resident of the White House. The fear of critics and public action forums is that such extensive Presidential involvement in matters normally considered legislative issues can easily lead to a quasi-dictatorial control our ancestors fought and died to prevent.

Section 3. He shall from time to time give to the Congress information of the state of the union, and recommend to their consideration such measures as he shall judge necessary and expedient, he may, on extraordinary sessions of occasions, convene both houses, or either of them, and in case of disagreement between them, with respect to the time of adjournment, he may adjourn them to such Time as he shall think proper; he shall receive ambassadors and other public ministers; he shall take care of that the laws be faithfully executed, and shall Commission all officers of the United States.

COMMENT: Again we have a statement of empowerment in the Executive Branch with little or no specificity. If misused or abused by the President, what prohibitions or limitations exist to hinder any such potential action?

Section 4. The President, Vice President and all civil officers of the United States, shall be removed from office on impeachment for, and conviction of treason, bribery or other high crimes and misdemeanors.

COMMENT: Here we are tasked to comment on a subject that in recent months during this writing has become one of the most controversial and at times most vitriolic in much of the discourse by both proponents and opposition. That is the interpretation of the specific words, "treason", "bribery", "high crimes" and particularly "misdemeanors."

To those in vehement opposition to the current holder of the Presidency impeachment is not only allowed but immediately called for. To others, accusations referring to the various misdeeds enumerated in Section 4 of Article II are grounds for some method of the individual's automatic disqualification for the office. Whatever the eventual outcome of this highly acrimonious barrage from both the opposition political party and the media, history tells us such an action has been rarely used and impotent in achieving its supporter's desire.

Andrew Johnson who gained the presidency at the assassination of newly reelected Abraham Lincoln was impeached but avoided removal by one vote. The charges included some petty disagreement of the appointment of one of the desired public offices at that time. William Jefferson Clinton faced removal for his accused dalliance with a young female intern while in office. His trial also resulted in no removal. It does demonstrate the difficulty in bringing impeachment actions and the problem in actually proving the elements sufficient for removal at the eventual trial. Since the entire impeachment process is rather lengthy and tedious in its process, I leave a further and more detailed description or discussion of the procedure to the writings and comments of others.

Suffice to say, until there is specificity built into an amended Section 4 of Article II, this disagreement of the actual meaning or legal substance of the disputed terms will remain. The currently extended and at times somewhat chaotic nature of the selection and campaigning of candidates for that high office, we need to remember altering those results – or removal - is a matter needing very serious review and deliberate consideration. True it is a blade that can be used to rid what might be viewed as a method to cleanse administrative impropriety or remove flaws in leadership but it remains a double edged blade.

● ● ●

ARTICLE III

Section 1. The judicial power of the United States shall be vested in one Supreme Court and in such in theory or courts as the Congress may from time to time ordain and establish. The Judges, both of the Supreme Court and inferior courts, shall hold their offices during good behavior, and shall, at stated times, receive their services a compensation, which shall not be diminished during their continuance in office.

COMMENT: It is accepted the Supreme Court has from its inception, been empowered to invalidate acts of the executive and legislative branches or subordinate bodies based on their finding or opinion that said act or action is in violation of the Constitution. It is agreed the judiciary at all levels must be ever vigilant in their findings that they follow neither social proclivities nor attempts to lead social thinking. Critics now contend this desired prudence has been notoriously absent in numerous legal findings over the past several decades.

There has become a powerful demand for justification within existing law of every such act. This becomes a veritable "Damocles Sword" handing over every proposed rule or law or action by the other two branches. A sword considered by many as the safeguard against a consolidation of power in one or the other branch. Contended by its supporters to be a method by which the former monarchial rule will never occur. In retrospect however, membership on the court and their views favoring the greater right or the more influenced left, had caused rumbles within that selection process even unto the term of FDR and his supposed "court packing" effort.

For many, the development of lower or as earlier phrased "inferior courts" has eased that contention somewhat, but never to the point they be totally eliminated. Although we speak of the many issues that have arisen since our founding and still perpetuate argument and political rancor, one fact exists. The Supreme Court does not address any issue until that issue has been shaped by law and thus can be reviewed as to its status within or in conflict with the constitution. The High Court cannot be expected to realistically review every decision made by lower courts unless the issue, formed into a law, has the need to be subjected to close scrutiny as to its constitutional intersection. It is the right and responsibility of the lower local, district, state and appellate judicial bodies to prepare the landscape on which the High Court is required to at least take notice of a judicial request and potentially submit it to its docket.

Despite it's often disregarded actions as they seem for many the concern of others, a serious contention still exists among many observers of the High Court's actions at times. Is it possible the Supreme Court has exercised and contended more power than the founders ever envisioned or desired. It has been said the opinion of the Court, rather than the facts presented and apparent to many, becomes the law. Is there any method, either voiced in the Constitution or by congressional mandate that can overturn any decision seeming to be both illogically reached or in definite breach of the public's interest? Have we endowed one of the three branches of government with unassailable powers to conduct our legal and societal affairs as only they see fit? Some will contend that freedom of legislative movement is the prerogative of the masses. Others feel, as supposedly so did our founding Fathers, a method of legal restraint must shadow the potential for legislative excess or impropriety.

Been recognized by the legal pundits who discourse on such matters that Federal judges have often become the weathervane of potential high court action. They influence far too much the final resolution of potential constitutional issues or in some instances literally affect societal norms.

Section 2. The judicial power shall extend to all cases, in law and equity, arising under this Constitution, the laws of the United States and treaties made, or which shall be made, under their Authority;-to all cases affecting ambassadors, other public ministers and consuls;-to all cases of Admiralty and Maritime jurisdiction; to controversies to which the United States shall be a party;-to controversies between two or more states;-between a State and citizens of another state;-between citizens of the same State claiming lands under grants of different states, and between a State, or the citizens thereof, and foreign states, citizens or subjects. Three the trial of all crimes, except in cases of impeachment, shall be by jury, and such trial shall be held in the State where the said crimes shall have been committed; but when not committed within these any State, the trial shall be at such Place or places as the Congress may by Law have directed.

The Supreme Court is equal in its position in the governmental triumvirate. Regardless of its human proclivities or debatable decisions, it must stand as the ultimate recourse the citizen has when containing or rigorously defending those aspects of the Constitution they look to for a clear definition of their rights and protections. Thus, the nomination and eventual acceptance of any individual to the high bench must be as the result of deliberative counsel and sincere desire to best protect the rights of the citizenry. Yet, it has long been the tool by which administrations have attempted to sway future decisions in a manner more fitting their political or personal agenda. As long as these selections are under the control of political influence, the nation must only hope that whomever rises to the High Court will have the personal and ethical strength to withstand such biased overtures that will knock at their door.

It must be understood that although laws are made by congress and submitted to the President for approval or the right of veto, legislatures come and go with each election period. The same for the occupant of the White House. As a result any such legislation can and is often either renewed or simply eliminated by a majority vote. Yet when the ever constant question of liberty involving individual and group rights comes to the fore, the Supreme Court is still the final arbiter of what the expression liberty really means.

Section 3. Treason against the United States, shall consist only in levying war against them, or in adhering to their enemies, giving them aid and comfort. No person shall be convicted of treason unless on the testimony of two witnesses to the same overt act, or on confession in open court. The Congress shall have the power to declare the punishment of treason, but no attainder of treason shall work corruption of blood, or forfeiture except during the life of the person attainted thereof.

COMMENT: In any discussion of the American judiciary system, be it the high court or some local magistrate, the question of potential bias comes to the fore. Particularly with the expression "treason" and the definition attributed that act by the framers of the document. Today that word is bandied constantly. It is used with abandon to classify any action by one individual or group when said action is considered grounds for removal or further legal repercussion.

With it rises the constant demand that judges at all levels adhere to the law as has been written, and precedent as has been time-tested and found both viable and directed toward the best interest of all who will appear before the bar of justice. On paper, the law appears purer and most simple. The law was originally conceived to reveal what is the right or wrong of an incident or claim or perceived wrong between mankind and policies of administrative bodies. Disposition of Justice is what the people allow those in power to administer. The courts are the protectors of the Constitution and as such must be the constant guardians of individual rights and their liberties. The might of the majority must be tempered by the proper interpretation of the law and to do less is in itself a violation of the doctrine upon which this country was founded and has striven so long to maintain.

Accompanying this responsibility must be the assurance that the minority opinion or claim is sufficiently represented. But, that the dissident voices are not allowed to abuse the very laws designed for their protection and valid right to seek redress and resolution of their position. Since the rule of law is the work of humans, thus its flaws must be understood and corrected in a proper manner when encountered. The conscientious intent of any legal ruling should not be limited to the supporters but rather, must be given for review and commentary by its critics.

Judicial officials who stand for election at prescribed times, are subject to societal and political pressures involved in every matter brought before them. Those receiving lifetime appointments, including the Supreme Court, are free to vary in ideology or insist on implementing their particular philosophy without concern for administrative recrimination or electoral recall, except in the case of specific misdeeds or causes.

It is regrettable that in numerous instances involving the Supreme Court of the land and a number of state high courts, wearers of the robes have in the minds of some, tended to institute public policy through their rulings or lack thereof. They move to interact within the language of existing law to alter its original purpose by defining the language without recourse by the legislatures that created such laws. This petty interference and directed incursion into areas not of their mandated authority, has tainted the purpose of this third branch of our government from local to the high benches.

We have been taught, and the dictum inculcated into any discussion of the Constitution, that there are the three distinctive rights. The right of the individual citizen, what is commonly referred to as States' rights, and the rights granted both Congress and the Executive Branch to have a recognized position to act under certain circumstances. I would submit there is an appearance of attempting to create policy and at times affect the normal implementation of existing law prior to appropriate constitutional review through the judicial system. Until this potential, never envisioned in formulating the Constitutional standards, is diminished and the court relegated to its established responsibility, this unacceptable interference in both legislative and executive functions will continue. The power of tenure must not be allowed to impinge on the legislative rights of Congress and those powers granted the Executive Branch. If this continues, I would suggest the following:

"Any decision of the Supreme Court that in fact or essence alters the intent or effect of a legislative action, shall be referred back to same legislative body for correction of those aspects or elements ruled to be in violation of the Constitution. That such ruling shall not be declared or inferred as being a newly phrased or structure alteration of the law in question. Such rights to correct, reformulate, and return to legislative consideration shall be that only of Congress."

The Judiciary Act of 1789 ostensibly created the format for which the judicial organization of our country was first developed. "Marbury v Madison, was instrumental in espousing the now apparently ingrained role of the high court. That matters before the court must not originate there but first be a matter of litigation in the lower courts and their findings being appealed then reached a potential level of consideration by the Supreme Court. Chief Justice John Marshall in 1804, basically outlined the premise by which actions of the lower courts would reach this highest body. However, not everyone agreed with his contention that the founders of the Constitution desired diversity in judicial review where the Supreme Court would become the last resort in such matters. However, there remain those who feel state law must have a greater preponderance in the final resolution of most legal contestations.

A rising opinion is that the state courts reflect the will of the people. Yet it is to the High Court many feel compliance to the current law of the land must be finally determined. Furthermore, that state courts are as sensitive to apprehension involving variations in legal interpretations and allows that the highest court is not the only guardian of that concern. Regrettably, the political control of appointment and election to various lower benches has qualified that insistence on total neutrality before the law.

● ● ●

ARTICLE IV

Full faith and credit shall be given in each State to the public acts, records, and judicial proceedings of every other state. And the Congress may by general laws prescribe the manner in which such acts, records and proceedings shall be proved, and the effect thereof.

COMMENT: Because of the insistence of varied legislative and governmental agencies, many records and reports of operations and litigations have often been kept sealed – a method to secure their nature and prevent unauthorized access. However, through the Freedom of Information Act (FOIA), increasingly, many long hidden materials have been released. Still, with a growing pseudo media claim for journalistic freedom, such bits and pieces of heretofore secreted documents and findings have become easy fodder for expansion of their purpose and intent far beyond fact. It has been said by some that journalism today is a jungle wherein predator and purveyor are often disguised under the same First Amendment rights. Transparency was loudly proclaimed as a hallmark of a former President's campaign rhetoric. Yet, the veil of obfuscation seemed quickly dropped in place, so that today the citizen has once more been excluded from the "holy of the holies" in the governmental temple to make broad use of biblical subjectivity.

Section 2. The citizens of each State shall be entitled to all privileges and immunities of citizens in the several states. A person charged in any State with treason, felony, or other crime, who shall flee from Justice, and be found in another state, shall on demand of the executive authority of the state from which he fled, be delivered up, to be removed to the State having jurisdiction of the crime. No person held to service or labor in one state, under the laws of thereof, escaping into another, shall in consequence of any Law or regulation therein, be discharged from any such service or labor, but shall be delivered up on claim of the party to whom such service or Labor may be due.

Section 3. New states may be admitted by the Congress into this Union; but no new State shall be formed or erected within the jurisdiction of any other State; nor any State be formed by the Junction of two or more states, or parts of states, without the consent of the legislatures of the states concerned as well as of the Congress the Congress shall have power to dispose of and make all needful rules and regulations respecting the territory or other property belonging to the United States; and nothing in this Constitution shall be so construed as to prejudice any claims of the United States, or of any particular state.

Section 4. The United States shall guarantee to every State in this Union a Republican form of government, and shall protect each of them against invasion; and on application of the Legislature, or of the executive (when the Legislature cannot be convened) against domestic violence.

Additionally, there is increasing clamor by certain elements to add the distant island Puerto Rico and the Washington D.C. area as fully embodied states. Practical or political, both issues bring forth a plethora of potential problems. Puerto Rico has its own disclaimer in the form of anti-US groups who demand their own sovereignty. Washington D.C. is the national capitol site and location for a great majority of governmental operations. Who then benefits when a large portion of all activities are literally tax exempt as being government in nature? Who then supports their common needs, public facilities, utilities, transportation and on and on? Would such a state designation be merely a method for the political party in power to have a secured electorate, at least until that balance of power would shift with the next election? With statehood, Congressional representation would incur giving rather large political influence to one area still in the throes of argued self-determination. And to another, even greater power in the administration of both their local and the national government. Much like being both judge and jury in any matters involving objective decision making.

●●●

ARTICLE V

The Congress, whenever two thirds of both houses shall deem it necessary, shall propose amendments to this Constitution, or on the application of the legislatures of two thirds of the several states, shall call a convention for proposing amendments, which in either case, shall be valid to all intents and purposes, as part of this Constitution, when ratified by the legislatures of three fourths of the several states, or by conventions in three fourths thereof, as the one or the other mode of ratification may be proposed by the Congress; provided that no amendment which may be made prior to the year One thousand eight hundred and eight shall in any manner affect the first and fourth clauses in the ninth section of the first article; and that no state without its consent, shall be deprived of its equal suffrage in the Senate.

●●●

● ● ●

ARTICLE VI

All debts contracted and engagements entered into, before the adoption of this Constitution, shall be as valid against the United States under this Constitution, as under the Confederation.

This Constitution, and the laws of the United States which shall be made in pursuance thereof; and all treaties made, or which shall be made under the authority of the United States, shall be the supreme law of the land; and the Judges in every State shall be bound thereby, anything in the Constitution or laws of any State to the contrary notwithstanding.

The Senators and Representatives before mentioned, and the members of the several state legislatures, and all executives and judicial officers, both of the United States and of the several states, shall be bound by oath or affirmation, to support this Constitution; but no religious test shall ever be required as a qualification to any office or public trust under the United States.

COMMENT: Here we note in the last sentence of Article VI, one of the most recent national political campaigns, an evident hypocrisy in both the media and opposing entities. Whether it be the past demonizing years ago of Presidential candidate Al Smith, the Catholic and the constant query as to John F. Kennedy's Catholicism or the birthright of Barack Hussein Obama, the fact remains. We have been and remain a Christian/protestant based society until an increase of other differing theologies and doctrine should become the majority of the population. The election of a recent President, at the time of this writing, was considered monumental in our country's electoral history as he was of mixed African American and Caucasian ethnicity. But again, he was of a declared protestant denomination.

Yet, were he Catholic or Jewish, would that sense of equality have existed? His opponent at his reelection bid four years later, was a member of the Church of Jesus Christ of Latter Day Saints – Mormons. That signaled a vitriolic outpouring from a number of sources, regrettably, some of those very organizations long declarers that all peoples are equal without caveat of personal preferences. The religious test remains part and particle of any election campaign review. The nature of any individual's past marital affiliations, economic status and long past views on certain social issues still shadows any potential candidate. While in contradiction to this article's definitive prohibition, it remains one of our country's dirty little procedural secrets constantly abused by a media well protected by the constitution they so often declare as outdated and irrelevant.

Today, another veritable fly in the ointment of those demanding total impartiality could be the possible entry of an individual into the presidential race who is a declared adherent to the Islamic faith, a Muslim who states his or her obeisance to the teachings of the Qur'an. A document that within its dialogue espouses the insistence on Sharia law as versus the present system of legal interpretation utilized in this country since its founding. Furthermore, what if this individual has stated in print and verbally over the years his or her acceptance of the denial of religious freedom to other faiths and the consideration of those as infidels and subject to annihilation. At what point does an assurance that the successful candidate will be fully compliant and subject to the Constitution become a verifiable condition for acceptance of that position. The Christian-Judeo concept was the basic premise in the foundation of our nation. Does the entry of a Chief Executive in such a powerful position in the administration of the primary laws and structure of our country place religious freedom as interpreted in the First Amendment in conflict with this section of the Article VI prohibiting any religious test for the office of President or Vice President?

● ● ●

ARTICLE VII

The ratification of the conventions of nine states shall be sufficient for the establishment of this Constitution between the states so ratifying the same.

COMMENT: With this declaration we now begin the review of the occasional tweaking that many have demanded over the years or, by circumstance and crisis, were required. These are those additions and alterations officially designated as "Articles of Amendment to the Constitution; but in the past century, more simply referred to as Amendments.

Expectedly, it is the First Amendment that brings forth the plethora of comment by strict proponents and opposition voices, often overshadowing other relevant parts of the Constitution. It is a paragraph of forty-five words that encompasses almost the entirety of proposed, expected and demanded freedoms for all residing within this country's borders. We will be taking a quick journey through the developing forest of initial growths of those sturdy trunks that comprised the basic structure of the document.

As we travel on we will take note of the many road signs and warnings one is likely to see when moving along the route to a desired location. In this instance, that destination is a fuller understanding of this truly unique undertaking by our founding Fathers. The linguistic sign posts are placed to bring to the reader's attention those changes, at times quite dramatic, in the original phraseology. Many still attempting to determine the meaning of the document authors.

If the history of our country's beginning and the tenuous periods of social, economic and political change are of little or no interest, then perhaps you will not wish to continue. Hopefully you will strive on just a bit further. It takes a conscious desire to understand a simple element of this current national status that at times can test the best of an individual's acumen in such matters. This part of the discussion will track where we rose from the chains of monarchial control to the freewheeling personal liberty advocated in today's multiplying ideological cacophony. It should be the duty of every citizen to have the presence of mind whenever claims or demands for immediate change or variance rises concerning the Constitution, regardless of how innocuous or well meaning. Then comes the hope that you will continue reading the detail of the Bill of Rights. Relatively a brief look at them, in the light of discovery, as to how we rose from a disparate foundation to the most influential power in the modern world.

Let us now start where any trip is initiated _ at the beginning - as we begin the review of the Amendments to the Constitution in what is termed the "Bill of Rights." It must be cautioned that alteration of any type to the original document is a lengthy and potentially tenuous process. It has been reported that well over 11,500 proposals to amend the United States Constitution have been proffered since 1789. It is further reported that around 200 such proposals are offered by members of Congress during each term. It must be noted that proposed amendments can be adopted and eventually sent to the individual states for ratification either by a two-thirds majority vote in both houses of Congress or by a national convention called for by Congress for such a purpose. However, it can occur only after application, *request,* of two-thirds of the state legislatures which is currently 34 states. To become part of the Constitution, an adopted Amendment must be *ratified* by either the legislatures of three-fourths of the states (currently 38) within a stipulated time period or by ratifying conventions in three-fourths of the states (38). At that point it becomes an operative part of the Constitution until further amended or negated by the same process. Thus we cannot lightly consider changing the document an action to be quickly or cavalierly taken by those in power.

However, a most important caveat, without the First Amendment it has been said all the rest are incidental and inconsequential in assuring our freedoms. Without this freedom of speech and religion, the position of the press and the right to petition and seek recourse, we would still be subject to potential tyranny were forces desiring dictatorial power to ever become dominant. So as we enter this realm of initial statements of governance and the eventual changes, it must be remembered each were brought about by the desire to modernize, to bring into the present, whatever the reasoning expressed at the time of each Amendment's proposal.

The First Ten Amendments, when first presented, were considered a Bill of Rights. All ten were proposed effective September 25, 1789 and eventually ratified, December 15, 1791. As we continue this part of the commentary, the date of each succeeding amendment's eventual ratification will be shown after its specific wording. It should be noted that the subsequent Amendments, from their initial proposal dates, took from three months, 8 days (the 26th Amendment allowing 18+ years to vote), to 202 years, 7-months, (the 27th Amendment, affecting Congressional salaries), first proposed, September, 1789 - ratified, May 5, 1992.

●●●

● ● ●

The Bill of Rights

•

The 1st Amendment

"Congress shall make no law respecting the establishment of religion, or prohibiting the free exercise thereof; or abridging the freedom of speech, or the press; or the right of the people peaceably to assemble, and to petition the Government for a redress of grievances."

RATIFICATION: First Ten Amendments – Bill of Rights, all proposed Sept. 25, 1789 & ratified Dec. 15, 1791

COMMENT: The First Amendment is, most simply stated, *the limitations placed on the government regarding those personal liberties felt so vital to a sincere evolvement of equality desired by our founding Fathers and for which so many have died to uphold.* No monarch or leader, regardless of how benevolent their supposed or proposed actions might be, should have the power or right to inflict on their subjects, denial of these basic freedoms. As overly broad as both the ultra-liberal or extremist conservative, the excessive activist and the radical discontent might brandish such unlimited rights as their escutcheon and as offensive or denigrating of traditional values as such freedom might seem, these are rights that must never be subjected to undue restraint or jacketed by rules intended to appease the supposed offended recipients.

There exist laws and regulations that provide certain restrictions that dwell principally on the purposeful destructive nature or evident intent by the declarer to deny others of equal rights or access. Any further limitations borders on infringement of the basic freedoms guaranteed in this and other parts of the Constitution. This writer shares the often dismayed and at times intense objection to many of the so-called freedom of speech advocates who revel in their total disregard for the sensitivities of others. Yet, it is the price we pay to assure we too are, when desired, recipients of the same freedom.

The 1ˢᵗ Amendment is possibly the most dynamic statement of purpose and intent ever written since the biblical prefacing statement, *"In the beginning."* So now, let us tear this very important declaration of mutual freedoms apart, segment by segment. Religion, its disparity among many societies and its demand by some to control others and its variance to generally accepted beliefs in certain areas, has resulted in more deaths throughout human history than any other cause of conflict. Let us approach these forty-four words, phrase by phrase.

"Congress shall make no law respecting an establishment of religion, or prohibiting the free exercise thereof;"

COMMENT: The men who wrote the basic language of the 1st Amendment referring to "establishment of religion" must have intended it to mean the financial support or sponsorship or any active involvement by any governing source. We recognize however that the Supreme Court has allowed certain cooperative arrangements including specific tax waivers and assistance in forms that eventually would aid such groups. Yet, judicial rulings maintained that any such involvement must not be seen as acceptance of position or support of any religious organization. It is in these somewhat convoluted interpretations that the argument as to what is the real meaning of "separation of church and state" remains. At the time the constitution in its original form, it was probably the general sentiment that Christianity was the dominant religious concept. That in itself has become the basis of most conflicting viewpoints as to the relationship between any religion and any government.

The question for years, why is even the mere mention or discussion of religion so divisive, so inflammatory when its right to exists is demanded and constitutionally enabled? Simple. It is the most personal and individually held emotional package of thought and opinion within the entire human psyche. It raises the flow of adrenalin and an increased motivation of the heart. Yet, to many, religion engenders suspicion, then distrust and eventually animosity toward practitioners or in other instances, those who would deny the tenets of a particular faith. Or when threatened by governmental or judicial intervention or interpretation, can create violent reaction against any supposed infringement or danger of suppression.

It must be understood that religion and politics have been forever entwined. Although the latter word is of more common use, the relationship has endured for millennium. Both elements seek the power to control their constituencies and then wish to dominate other dominions to expand their influence, either in control or propagation of a particular theology. Separating the two factions is impossible as they feed on each other so as to accomplish their individual goals however noble or banal. It is a relationship created in the depths of ambition and sustained through the naiveté of the people they serve or attempt to indoctrinate.

In the early days of our nation's development, freedom of religion was a paramount concern of our founding fathers. However, since most were protestant – ergo mostly Christian in a broad sense and expressed themselves in their manner of considering the newly proposed form of government – they were too often intolerant of any belief or expression in conflict with theirs. Thus the grant of such freedoms was limited and construed within a very narrow scope for years. Supreme Court Associate Justice Felix Frankfurter in his 1942 dissent in Jones v. Opeleika, 316 U.S. 584, spoke eloquently concerning certain municipal rules regarding Jehovah Witnesses religious materials sales. He wrote "The constitutional protection of religious freedom terminated disabilities; it did not create new privileges. It gave religious equality, not civil immunity. Its essence is freedom from conformity to religious dogma, not freedom from conformity to law because of any religious dogma...” We have been inundated by various religious ideologies, sects, cults and vague demands for their right to express their particular religious fervor in their own and sacrosanct manner and location.

This has become very evident with two examples. The small, disparate Topeka, Kansas church or sect that insisted on protesting at burials of military personnel who have died in action is not only abominable but, in this writer's opinion, also a direct use of the First Amendment as concerns both freedom from abridgement of religion and Freedom of Speech. They were a small, indistinct, psychologically twisted group, primarily populated by the pastor's extended family. The principle figure died in late 2014, and to date little more has been heard from the now ostensibly leaderless group. Regardless, their actions were despicable and stretched even the most liberal view of the extent of freedom of religion and its accompanying coverage of verbal and printed expositors. However they expressed their misdirected vitriol within the umbrella of free speech as is guaranteed in the First Amendment. When any group contending religious freedom based on this aspect of the First Amendment, seems to others to have crossed the line of decency and social decorum, as intolerable as it may be for many, theirs is protected speech. It is required in order to sustain the other rights as dictated therein.

Even more shocking and eventually creating a devastating incident, the infamous Jonestown vision of ersatz preacher Jim Jones. He rose from an earlier career as more community organizer than religious leader. Eventually he developed his Jonestown encampment in the jungles of Guyana where his apparent psychotic version of a safe haven for the ill-treated or lesser advantage membership of his self-endowed church resulted in the suicidal or forced deaths of 913 persons including Jones himself. Regrettably such ideological malcontents will, when criticized for their inane actions or cautioned by others, immediately declare theirs is a right to Freedom of Speech, also never to be abridged in any manner.

Yet, regardless of this protective veneer which I do not wish to see totally diminished, might we contemplate a variance to this potentially occasional insensitive use of religious incivility. Supreme Court Associate

Justice William O. Douglas wrote in the Engel v. Vitale, 370, US, 421 (1962); "If there is any fixed star in our constitutional constellation, it is that no official, high or petty, can prescribe what shall be orthodox in politics, nationalism, religion or other matters of opinion, or to force citizens to confess by word or act their faith therein." In summarizing the intent and substance for this clause in the Amendment, we must clarify what has become a misconception for past decades.

The phrase, "separation of church and state" does not appear in the Constitution, nor in any other founding document. The clause merely gives citizens the freedom to worship God without government interference. The actual use of the expression "citizen" has also become a bone of contention to some who will ascribe that term only to native born or legally naturalized or legal resident individuals. But in the verbiage, and I believe the intent of the current law, it bestows certain freedoms on all those present within the boundaries of our country and territories.

The "wall" concept arose from the thoughts of Thomas Jefferson, a later number of Justices and many assumed pundits. In Jefferson's letter in 1802 to the Danbury Baptist Association of Connecticut, he used a metaphor, "a wall of separation" when responding to the association's reference to their "weekly worship services in the House Chambers of the U.S. Capital building." Oddly, although that expression does not appear in the U.S. constitution, it apparently did in the constitution of the old USSR, Union of Soviet Socialist Republics.

A portion of the 1st Amendment prohibits the government from entering the field of religious development or control. This is the wall, supposedly referenced by Jefferson that shelters those desiring to proclaim and practice a particular theology free from hindrance or interception by those in power. To consider that wall to have no accessible points for proper administration of the social welfare and protection of the lesser informed public, is to blind oneself from the need to assure such religious freedom does not allow persecution or disadvantage of other religions. Supreme Court Associate Justice Sandra Day O'Connor wrote, regarding the establishment of religion clause, "Government should not make one's religious belief or lack thereof relevant to one's standing in the political community." This appears to have been forgotten in the current and ignoble assault on one or more of the recent political contenders known religious beliefs. It is a contemptible move toward a biased atmosphere, regrettably too fostered by continuous media emphasis on that subject.

When one's persuasive efforts attempt to dominate or unreasonably affect the free expression or existence of another, it is the obligation of civil law to contain such actions. The freedom to believe as one wishes and practice one's singular theology is guaranteed; but it does not presume immunity from or disobedience to civil law or restraint from criminal behavior. Liberty, however defined or imagined, must be quantified by a societal discipline to accept those reasonable controls that allow all concerned to enjoy its benefits without deprivation of their own personal rights. We all desire that freedom of religion in its various forms shall be inviolable as regards its pursuit. I would at this time suggest a personal approach to the administration of the Freedom of religion and its corollary, Freedom of Speech.

"That it shall remain cognizant and responsible under the law as concerns any and all actions as a group or by its principle spokes-persons action to degrade, demean, attempt to persecute or otherwise lessen the right to free expression as shall be enjoyed by all religious beliefs. And furthermore, to assure that any such religious groups, who shall overtly or with proven intent, attempt to subvert its tax position or legal existence shall face all penalties and legal recourse as shall affect all others committing similar or like offenses or activities. In addition, any religion claiming priority to facilities and demands for services that create an imbalance in the operational structure and administration of any public entity, shall be prohibited from requiring said special advantage on the basis that denial of such demands is in conflict with their religious practice."

We cannot allow either the courts or the congressional representation to continually secularize everything which they assert has religious basis, overtones or initiation. Such attempts or demands fly in the face of the history of our founding. Whether one is an adherent to any particular theology or doctrine, our beginning was based in a religious covenant that remains, however an anathema, to the more liberal element in the political skein of our society. There remains a sensitive and workable separation of church and state to assure the equality so much a part of our current structure. To allow condemnation, prohibition and refusal to accept tradition and long held values by a majority of the nation is to engender sure rejection. To demand secularism to the maximum is to deny a heritage held so dearly and fought for so vigorously over the years to survive.

I now am forced to bring into a brighter light, the issue of increasing demands by certain Islamic groups in our country to provide special religious oriented privileges and services. In many instances, compliance with such demands can in itself be identified as budgetary and administrative disadvantage and/or hindrance in effective operation of the facilities in question. We are being besieged by insistence that Sharia law become an integral part of many judicial decisions. Demanded special facilities and never before required perquisites have become the mantra of a religion, that in its nearly fourteen centuries since its inception, has never allowed such preferences or special exceptions for non-believers – infidels as such persons or groups are termed.

Religion is the balm of comfort to many and the resort of the bereaved, the depressed and the emotional wanderer to seek resolve for personal needs and questions. It is a form of self-examination and ease of inner turmoil that is to many a release from the prison of their personal doubts and armor against the demons of their imagination or circumstances. It cannot be a refuge for those desirous of condemning other beliefs or vehicles to dominate and pursue activities detrimental to guaranteed individual liberties. Equality is a broadly interpreted term. It hides within its structure the opportunity for some to demand a greater share of benefit and service not available to, or provided others. Religion is a path of belief and direction taken by its adherents. It is not a tool for self-aggrandizements and the accomplishing of revenue collection well beyond the specific religion's operational, administrative and charitable requirements, as has occurred with several current mega-church activities.

We have been exposed over the past several centuries by those who would proclaim a direct confluence with God. It is a claim that their steadfast commitment emanates from the highest authority. It is this proclaimed divine inspiration that too often leads supplicants later feeling they have been led to a place or position quite removed from normalcy and reason. Radio at first and then television, has become the modern day Chautauqua and revival tents of past. Yet it is the freedom to expound, to declare or to debate whatever philosophic or theological dogma they wish is also a safeguard against retaliation as provided by the First Amendment and freedom of religious belief.

During the past few decades, the controversial and often contentious debate as to separation of church and state has blurred the original intent of that part of the Amendment. Until there is definitive qualification and categorical rules of conduct as to the relationship between a private undertaking of a religious nature and its involvement or association with a public funded and or controlled activity, this dispute will merely grow like the rot on a weathered and untended house. We shall discuss this aspect of constitutional confusion later. Yet, let us not forget U.S. Supreme Court Associate Justice Hugo Black's opinion regarding the "establishment clause," when he commented that it "Rests on the belief that a union of religion and government tends to destroy government and degrade religion."

The right to practice one's own religious structure and ideology and the ability to divorce those beliefs from any required adherence to, has been more recently highlighted with the rise of a presidential candidate who happened to be a member of the Church of Jesus Christ of Latter Day Saints, commonly referred to as Mormons. For older readers this will seem to harken back to the 1928 presidential campaign when former New York Governor, Al Smith, the first Roman Catholic to receive serious consideration for that office faced the same question as to the possible effect of his religious conviction on his administration of the laws of our country.

This type of less spoken but still whispered potential for an external influence shadowed John F. Kennedy's campaign in 1960. Some will argue that Smith and Romney's religion was in part the reason for the defeat of each in the national election. Whatever the basis for such contention, and as improper any such consideration when viewing any candidate, it appears the religion of any applicant will remain, however indistinct in speech or action infer a hint. Regrettably it may still remain part of unspoken campaign rhetoric for years to come.

I have purposely spent much verbiage on this subject because it is so often the most common denominator of reference when anyone discusses the Constitution. To many who espouse a religious preference, it is a cherished and vital freedom. A recent situation where an elected County clerk in part of Kentucky refused to issue marriage licenses to those of the same sex desiring this documentation in preparation for their wedding of one another. Although the Supreme Court had recently upheld such a right, the clerk refused, stating it was in violation of her religious beliefs. Jailed for her refusal, later released, her action became the center of a controversial discussion of the right to disallow any law on the basis of religious objection has continued. The point of this particular incident is the question, can an elected official who swore an oath to up hold the Constitution and current law of the land, so object on the basis of adherence to specific religious convictions? A thorny and as yet unresolved situation.

To the opposite end of the spectrum are those who consider religious persuasion as an impermissible interference in the primary responsibility of government and would demand that all religious references and ceremonial involvement, particularly in schools and public events, be terminated. It is a contest neither can win nor lose results only in divisiveness. Justice William O. Douglas may have most succinctly marked the thin margin between the religious advocate and the more liberal opposition when he said, "Men may believe what they cannot prove", Denis v. U.S. 354 U.S. 494 (1951).

"or abridging the freedom of speech,"

COMMENT: Why were our Founding Fathers so intent on stipulating this specific freedom to initiate the first addition to their basic declaration of personal equality? Because the original inhabitants from Europe who formed the nucleus of a later civilization, came to the new world specifically to be free to worship in their own way. Thus, this ingrained desire was soon coupled by the freedom to express their beliefs on other subjects, including the current form of governing or the controlling power of administration of basic social activities. To expand their small group of adherents through written and verbal speech was critical to the advancement of their position. Today, that is the basis of any call for, clamor, demand or demonstration by, those insisting on equality in the forum of protestation or public declaration.

The initial exemption was considered "yelling fire" in a crowded theater." Additionally, there are specific preclusions to freedom of speech encompassed in the laws of slander and libel. The question continues as to what, if any limitation, should be put on speech in its verbal, written, or pictorial representation by whatever form? Should production, overtly or directly intended bring into public view insult, demeaning or denigrating commentary or assault against the beliefs of others, politically, religious or physical? Cartoons and improvisational skits, in theaters or televised, have been the focus of many who contend there must be borders across which so called adherents of unbridled free speech should be prohibited from crossing under pain of legal redress. Now these two rather wordy sentences may seem excessive in their declaration but they do, to this writer, encompass many of the complaints by some against what has been so common today. The accused disparaging and actual mockery of another's religious or political conviction or persuasion, e.g. the escalating public controversy over a violent attack against a noted French publication for contended cartoon insults of the Islamic prophet Mohammed.

This is not the first time there have been violent reactions to one individual or one group's use of their constitutionally guaranteed freedom of speech to literally vilify a targeted religious or political entity or position. Yet, if even the merest restraints are put in place regarding the more objectionable and vile speech, by whatever form, would this be just the beginning for eventual measurable diminishing of that treasured right? This is a sensitive and extremely politically fraught area of discussion. It has been and will continue to be debated in most vociferous terms for years to come and cannot be resolved in this dissertation.

In Justice Black's majority decision in Emerson v. Board of Education, 330 U.S. 1, 675.ct 504 (1947), the presumed "wall of separation" between the state and the church, whatever theology, became a pseudo form of Constitutional law. That misconception has been discussed earlier. It must be understood by those so bent on erasing any mention of God or the supposed assumption of endorsement by allowing prayer at public meetings, that unless more cogent reasoning can be proffered, their demands border on denial of the rights encompassed within this Amendment. The union of the church and the state was an aspect of total control which the dissenters of the mid-17th Century wanted abolished. They wanted freedom to worship in their own way, but not at the behest or within any rule by any governing authority. (I.e. Church of England -- State sponsored religion.)

Existing however is the clamor of the ultra-evangelical right who depict anyone questioning any religious input as demonic and "un-American." Hopefully, this is the voice of a misled few who constantly cloud the vision of a suitable separation of church and state and the need to allow both viewpoints their fair share of vocalization and protestation. Across the imagined street from this diametrical division are those who would have any mention of God or religious belief banned from any public pronouncement. It is this scarcity of compromise from both sides that continually erupts into public displays of asininities that beggars the imagination of rational society. At this time there exists a minimal prohibition to any totally uninhibited expression of opinion or statements that impugn or directly libel or slander the name, reputation, character or position of another individual.

Aside from this desire to assure speech is never limited to any degree that might inhibit expression of any dissenting viewpoint, one major flaw in that concept still exists. That of the immunity enjoyed by members of

Congress in their statements made while on the floor of either the Senate or House of Representatives. Here, the most egregious examples of possible slander in speech and libel by placement in the Congressional Record have occurred over the past two plus centuries. In this writer's opinion, there must be an equal facility, one for they who issue such commentary under the cloak of Congressional immunity, and the target of such commentary who either feel they have been injured or legally slandered or defamed. Now we again suggest an optional approach to the language of that particular segment of Article I.

"That any statement made by a member of Congress from the floor of that body, be subject to the same required truthfulness, absence of falsity and acceptable under the laws that protect each and every citizen from libel and/or slander. And that the particular speaker of such statements shall not be absolved of any eventual liability or shall be allowed safeguard from recourse through the protection of immunity and such declared injured party may pursue reasonable redress through the process of civil law."

Thus, elected officials would be cautioned to add factual element and required truthfulness in such statements or claims issued from legislative chambers. And that they be subject to the same legal recourse all citizens have, to protect name, reputation and character if such remarks rise to the level of legal rebuttal. To minimize such legal action, the offending member of Congress be required, when such statements are found to be false or without any reasonable basis of fact, to publicly and from the floor of the particular legislative body, issue a sufficient verbal and written apology for such statements and such be directed to the target of such remarks. Such apology to be both entered into the official Congressional Record and publicized through whatever means can be used to rectify the situation and inform the general public of such retraction and apology.

We elect our fellow citizens to office so that they may put forward the wishes, intents and wants of their constituency. Not to consider themselves immune from the same obligation and potential legal redress all citizens must face for intemperate, false or misleading expression, verbally or through the written word. The legislative branch of our government does not have imperial powers. They cannot shed the responsibility for civility, truthfulness and ethical behavior so expected of all other Americans. Their immunity serves as just an unadorned cloak of hypocrisy. Too many innocent individuals unconnected to the matters, instances or described activities have been permanently injured, their reputation and credibility destroyed or seriously damaged by such indiscriminate and improper use of the congressional immunity shelter.

"or of the Press;

COMMENT: The claim "We have freedom of the press" immediately creates a cacophony of indignation and excess of denying journalistic misconduct we must endure every time the media in all forms might become suspect or are revealed for bias and purposeful misfeasance in their ethical obligations. A free press is the conduit for total information and critical oversight of any and all governmental operations, local, state and nationally subscribed. Before continuing further, let me clarify my basic belief regarding this part of the First Amendment. "Unless government is not subject to constant review, subjection of the governed will result." But with this supposedly unlimited access to every move of those in elected or economic power, there comes an obligation and conscious awareness of the rights of those who have become target of such media inquiry. Regrettably this is a pledge too often disregarded in today's frenzy to explore and expose without factual substance.

The extensive growth of multi-faceted media approaches, network and cable TV, newspapers, magazines, periodicals and the surge in electronic output, "blogs", "Facebook" and "Twitter" and "YouTube", just to name the current principle outlets, has further expanded the opportunity for diverse opinion, unjustified statements and proliferation of purported facts without legitimate verification. A thin line divides freedom of expression as supposedly the hallmark of Constitutional liberty with unfettered propaganda and falsity. Where does legal oversight become a safeguard against impropriety in output by media or the oft-described shadow of the "Big Brother" mentality? Might I present a suggested caveat to this freedom of the press?

"That the media in its many organized, structured forms, shall observe the laws regarding slander and/or libel and shall be required to respond to any and all claims that reports, statements, issuance of purported facts, be subject to review and if found to be inaccurate, false or overtly misleading, shall be recanted and an appropriately visible and broadly distributed correction shall be issued at the earliest time practical after revelation of any such inaccuracy or falsity. And if continuing under the umbrella of their personal interpretation of that aspect of the First Amendment guaranteeing their right to expression without control, criminal penalties could be assessed if found that such continuing utterances further denies the civil rights of the targets of such media commentary or pursuit."

We must have a free press. We must continue its protection from governmental or personally engendered control or utilization of standards that merely mirror social fads or personal grievances. Yet, as an ensign of an informed public to insure continuance of the public interest and freedoms, we would not allow this too often fouled pennant to become dirtied by the subjectivity of those with personal agendas. Fairness, objectivity of approach, and clarity as to sources and the intent to be unbiased, should be the escutcheon of the true journalists. All others should be required to initiate all commentary as personal opinion or directed viewpoint from specific sources or their employer.

During the early days of our country, journalism and all those who would use the written word to unveil corruption or malfeasance in government or politics, faced a dangerous time. The journalist was expected to merely repeat what had been told he or she. To attempt to bring the truth to light placed the writer in fear of retribution, socially and punitively. However, "times they have changed" to paraphrase an often used comment of years before. Today, almost all declared journalists, print or broadcast, news reporter or columnist, have forgotten both the process of the true reporter or the ethics inherent therein. Yet, we are required to uphold this consummate right guaranteed in the Constitution, for to disavow its intent, would allow potential dictatorial tyranny which we've fought for years to defend against here and abroad.

Unfortunately, too many members of what was once such an honored profession, have in fact become so enamored of their status as to occasionally indulge in might be termed, "initiators of factual illusion." Moving ever farther to an evident strongly liberal bent, they today seem to perform their functions by purveying a version of actual events, regardless of the misleading or inaccurate manner presented. It is doubtful that a sense of morality in procedure will ever again permeate the professional journalist ranks. Credibility has become the whim of the listener or reader, depending on what opinion they originally held on any subject. So many members of the media have become veritable pawns of either certain national administrations, or when that is in conflict with their personal views, the leftist opposition. The shame is ours for allowing the ethically impotent to become the majority voice of the print and electronic information resources.

For any government to totally control the people without ongoing outcry, they must have a complicit media. It is only the revelation of misdeeds or the issuance of suspicion that first creates demand for further investigation. It is this continual search for the truth of every legislative or administrative action or statement that provides assurance the public welfare is being given the needed and constitutionally mandated attention. Regardless of any of the excesses that have and may occur in the future, the media must still be allowed unfettered access to any and all information sources regarding any and all government operations and actions. Other than the defined and accepted needs for national security as must be specific in its application, without the ability to puncture that often constructed veil of government secrecy our concept of freedom of information is in danger of becoming moot.

It was during the administration of President McKinley, and the initiation of the short-lived but politically altering Spanish-American War that changed the role of the media. From their traditional reportorial and investigative role they became more politically active. Whether the bane of some candidates, or the pawn of other political parties and ideologies, they became the printed and later broadcast power behind many administrations. The print power of William Randolph Hearst and his infamous dictate to his reporters at the scene of conflict, "I will create the war, you just report it," fashioned the framework that would become the mantra of the media. Since then, the biased involvement of print and broadcast journalists has impregnated the profession with excessive personal viewpoint. More so, during the past few decades, the overt support of doctrines and political actions going far beyond the ethical limits of the profession.

"or the right of the people peaceably to assemble, and to petition the Government for a redress of grievances."

COMMENT: This right has been the vehicle for more rioting and violent demonstrations than any other aspect of personal demands for this guarantee. Regrettably it is the uninformed, the emotionally immature, and those intent on self-gratification that has too often dictated the level of destruction and personal injury such protests have engendered. Yet, the right to demonstrate, to protest, ergo to assemble to present grievances cannot nor should not be limited within reason. It must remain an inherent right. Unfortunately occasions have arisen where peaceable demonstrations and protest gatherings have been exacerbated into more explosive situations by the excessive presence of far more law enforcement personnel than the nature of the event either required or was rationally necessary. The inability of some security forces to understand the nature of such events or the absence of the elements of potential violence has regrettably caused more harm that was justified. The has to be a recognition on both sides that the inclusion of peacefully protesting groups with those having no affiliation with the purposes of the group must be reviewed as to separating those intending damage, violence and terrorizing from the worthwhile nature of the original gathering.

"Those participating in the deleterious nature of demonstrations that escalate into periods of damage, destruction, personal assault on opponents and/or innocent bystanders, shall be considered terrorist in behavior if they pursue acts or methods that provoke and foster violence amongst themselves or by their actions as onlookers whether or not associated with the initial fomenters or organizers. That such charges and penalties incurred must also include any member of involved law enforcement who have either failed to fulfill their role in maintaining the peace and rights of the recognized protestors or themselves have committed unwarranted assault on any of the participants. And the penalties regarding those incarcerated as a result of their actions shall be the maximum allowed without contention of freedom to assemble or contended position of authority."

We are, in the main, a gathered society, unable to just distance ourselves from interaction with our fellow man. However, the use of this freedom to assemble has too long been the defense against the desire of others to demand justice for those injured or killed or property and material damage wreaked too often on innocent bystanders, merchants and law enforcement officials. Too often we have heard the remonstrance to complaints by consumers, constituency, or citizens simply requesting or demanding service that people are too sensitive to change or the process of carrying out such requests. The right "to petition the Government for a redress of grievances" has long been the bane of the employed, appointed, or elected official who is responsible for responding to such requests or demands.

Yet, it is this channel to resolution that must be maintained and enforced so as to provide quality and timeliness in the response process. Although time consuming, and in many instances possibly seeming an exercise in futility to properly satisfy certain complaints or requests, the procedure still requires a continuing refinement and structure. There should be an admonition to the ongoing insistence that "everything is or has been done" but the complainant is just whispering against the wind. I would suggest the following adjunct in the form of an admonition:

"The government at all levels, shall aggressively attend to the right of the citizen to seek redress of grievances in a timely and reasonably satisfactory manner. And that a permanent record shall be entered and maintained as to the resolution or final disposition of the matter. Furthermore, where shown that such exercise of such right has been ignored, overtly or inadvertently, or response delayed without reasonable consideration, or that appeal of any disposition has not been recorded or allowed, the offending official and/or governmental agency involved shall be held legally responsible and a new hearing by an impartial resource shall be granted within a reasonably timely manner and process."

It is the government's responsibility to attend to the needs and voice of its constituency. It can do no less than expend whatever energy and resources are needed to resolve disputes and reach out to the citizen to assure appropriate response. This is the true representative nature of a government, attuned to its fellow citizens. More importantly, it was the basis of consideration so thoroughly expressed by the documents writers. Sadly, to this writer, this is an attitude that has dwindled in importance in the minds of many who are and have been elected to confirm and uphold that original concept.

As comprehensive as the First Amendment is it must also be the cover for all the various minority groups, ethnic, and minority, economic, political and socially non-traditional sexual proclivities encompassed in the LGBT. They cannot be forced into a secondary status in order for the First Amendment freedoms to be truly everyone's right.

•

We now address one of the more hotly contested areas of individual rights as is encompassed in the 2nd Amendment of the Constitution.

The 2nd Amendment

A well-regulated Militia, being necessary to the security of a Free State, the right of the people to keep and bear arms shall not be infringed.

COMMENT: The declared anti-gun coalitions have long demanded that the private citizen be severely restricted in ownership of guns. The current coined term, "assault weapons," used to designate semi and automatic firing rifles, has become the code word for eliminating what most have felt is the primary essence of the Second Amendment. The absence of the word "person" or individual in this amendment is loudly declared by certain opponents as ample reason for its proposed abandonment. Even more recently certain members of academia have targeted the lack of the word "individual" in this amendment declaring it removes individual right as against the general supposition of a citizen militia. A professor of English at Utah's noted university, has seen fit to write that the absence of the word "person" totally defends his disagreement of the traditional interpretation of the Second Amendment. This academic acolyte of arcane thinking was quick to direct attention to Art. I, Sec.2, to validate his thesis. As if he failed to understand that any section of any document of historic but aging proportion can be interpreted in as many different ways as there are viewers.

Like too many of his Ivory Tower colleagues, this particular individual's call for relinquishment of personally owned firearms is in the opinion of his critics merely an attempt to deny the rights within the 2nd Amendment. To them it is both myopic in viewpoint and political campaign jargon rather than truly definitive controls that limit improper use yet retain the basic concept of the Amendment. That such forfeiture of this basic right by the common citizen to "bear arms" however broadly interpreted lacks recognition of the reality of a society rife with danger and ongoing threat. Furthermore I binds most academics and liberalists with a belief in their self-endowed wisdom of the true nature of society.

There is ample reason to limit access to certain high velocity weapons and extended ammunition magazines whose use and purpose seems beyond the need of the average citizen or even the avid hunter. However, to attempt removing the individual's right to bear arms rather than instituting reasonable conditions is tantamount to declaring open conflict with those who will fight such prohibition. Registration, universal background checks, and the close observance of those whose emotional imbalance creates a public danger are all merited measures. The sycophantic attitude of the politician to assuage the liberal left has too often created maelstroms of unneeded fodder for an already biased media.

The use of the word "militia", which my Oxford Dictionary of Common English, states as "a military force, especially one conscripted in an emergency and normally comprised of current members of the citizenry," is the only sole definition of the right to bear arms. To supporters of these rights, it is a word in concert with the expression "to militate against" or "to operate or work against". Thus, were a situation to arise wherein groups of citizens felt they were being threatened or intimidated or being oppressed in violation of their individual or composite liberties, they would have the right to resist as best they could within existing law. And under the worst circumstances, such advocates contend that without access to arms they would be defenseless against any comparable threat of tyranny or onslaught by organized groups or any government sponsored entity.

It is lamentable that certain diverse ideologies have created armed resistance both using the title "citizen's militia" thereby cloaking their possibly illegal intent and methods within this Amendment. This is where the line between authorize or substantially reasonable and improper or illegal becomes blurred. It will continue so long as adamant opposition seeks to take a more physical and/or violent approach in their demand for addition or elimination of particular goals. There will always be the confusion between the use of the expression "militia" and "the right of the people". Does one countermand the other? Does it require this right of an armed presence as it refers only to organized military, para-military or created and endowed law enforcement agencies?

Furthermore, that defense and protection of one's home and family and property is an endowed and constitutionally guaranteed right of every citizen. That without the right "to bear arms", the individual or community would find themselves at the mercy of those wishing harm, theft or destruction of those same citizens and communities. The courts have ruled that the word militia refers only to maintenance of a standing citizen army. But then again, is the existing standing army a citizen militia, as they are both comprised of those wishing to pursue a full-time occupation and those wishing to merely volunteer for a much shorter duration? As to the meaning of words, so much the fodder of academia in disagreement, we can never determine exactly what the writers of this particular amendment intended in the use of the two words, "keep" and "bear" arms. Does 'bear' mean the absolute right to carry firearms on one's person? To actually walk in public "bearing" such weapons? And as to 'keep' those same arms, does that allow any law or regulations, however well meaning, to prohibit ownership of any guns by citizens?" The writers of the Constitution used what they understood was Standard English at the time. Yet evolution has and will always occur; whether it be in languages used, social norms, or the world of science.

Again I must defer to those far more astute and expert in such specific language. I for one will maintain a personal belief in the language of the Constitution being what it is. If needing clarification, changes can be made as I have and will always contend, in a documented, legally allowed and appropriate manner. I must agree that there is a need for limits on such armament where the need or purpose is unclear or obviously without reasonable merit. So, what should be the criteria for owning such weapons? And to what degree should the government be permitted or allowed to restrict this ownership? Where do the gun collector and the avid hunter cross the line of acceptable possession by type and number and becomes a threat to others or the security of the public in general? At the time of this writing, a number of terribly tragic and brutal slayings of groups of innocent victims have occurred. With such a plethora of dastardly acts, in the main committed by those later proven to have serious emotional and mental problems, the cry arises to ban all weapons in the hands of non-military or law enforcement individuals. Radical proposals and excessive solutions are forthcoming in a torrent after such tragedies. Patience is the best rate of the trek to resolution of any such contentious and sensitive matter.

No one has the consummate answer. Here we are speaking to the very heart of the right of free movement and action so embedded in our early history. The basis of frontier psychology and the determined caricature of the lone figure facing the imponderables of an unknown future. The ultra-liberal, anti-gun lobby would have us believe that total abolition of private gun ownership would drastically reduce deaths by gunshot. The opponents counter that to do so is to leave the private citizen completely at the beck and call of the thief, the home invader, and all those who would do harm to that individual and his or her family and property. It stems far back into medieval times when those armed were in control and those without weaponry were considered the prey. Here we proffer the following addition to the current interpretation of this amendment.

"Collection of weaponry and both ownership and possession of legally acquired firearms shall be permitted insomuch as said individuals or groups permit inspection as to number and types by authorized law enforcement agents with use of a valid warrant and with advance notification to the owner. And that the state or federal government shall have the right to assess reasonable limits to the numbers and types of such weapons through a defined and reasonably constructed criteria designating when need or purpose exceeds normal considerations.

Furthermore, ownership of extensive numbers of weapons and ammunition shall be so identified and explained as to purpose on any registration of said weaponry. That those purporting to be legitimate collectors, retail weapons outlets, or recognized weapons producers or repair facilities, be willing to provide upon reasonable and warranted request an inventory of all such items in their possession or owned and located on other premises."

As with all such volatile subjects, it needs close scrutiny as relates to individual liberties in conflict with the general public interest. Regardless of which direction future gun control legislation moves, the criminal, the malefactor, the deranged or intending evil-doer can and will find firearms.

There are those who feed on this nefarious need and to imagine or even pretend total gun control can erase this ongoing threat are misguided and Pollyanna like in their thinking. The need for excessive armament, such as is exhibited in the growing cadre of what are often referred to as assault weapons, is beyond this writer's understanding.

Excessively large magazines for military styled automatic and semi-automatic weapons appear of little value to the true hunter and sportsman; Other than the fulfillment of some misguided attempt to assume the role of a fictionalized hero figure. Again, the right of the individual to legally own a firearm must be tempered by an understanding of the responsibility owed to one's family, associates, and the general public. To some, this right of possession is one of those inalienable rights espoused in the Constitution. Regrettably, as carrying and use of firearms were the normal element of early frontier, and later early urban life, the Founding Fathers may have never imagined the technology of firearms as has evolved over the years.

•

The 3ʳᵈ Amendment

No Soldier shall in time of peace be quartered in any house, without the consent of the Owner, or in time of war, but in a manner to be prescribed by law.

COMMENT: This has not been of concern to anyone expressing concern with or opinion of the U.S. Constitution since long after the Civil War. As long as any law, current, proposed or legislated in the future, retains the privacy of the individual citizen household, this article should remain inviolate in its content and intent. For the added safety of communities and protesting groups as a whole, could it not be further detailed as to the extent of "martial law" being enacted by either state or national authority? Although the ability to quell violence and/or the potential for human and property destruction is equally critical to the maintenance of the public good order, the right to be free from impingement on the freedom to protest in a reasonable and nonviolent manner becomes the overriding concern when implementing such armed reaction.

This next Amendment has provided both prosecution and defense efforts within the judicial process, the greatest opportunities and at times devastating setbacks in the history of modern jurisprudence for both parties in any legal confrontation. It has created volumes of court opinions at all levels. Its interpretation is so widely diverse as to confuse jurists, contesters, and proponents alike.

•

The 4th Amendment

The right of the people to be secure in their persons, houses, papers and effects, against unreasonable searches and seizures, shall not be violated, and no Warrants shall issue, but upon probable cause, supported by Oath of affirmation, and particularly describing the place to be searched, and the persons or things to be seized.

COMMENT: One of the more cherished freedoms, it provides a protection from unauthorized or unlawful access to one's person, property, or purchase. This was a liberty long coming to citizens of many other countries, to the extent, in many Middle-Eastern and Asian locations, this protection does not exist at all. The requirement that to enter your residence, to search your person or personal bags, etc., requires prior legal documentation, gives all the ability to feel far safer from intrusion. Yet that security, in many minds, includes the ownership of a defensive weapon. As one twit remarked, "unless you're carrying a properly filed warrant in your hand, beware as I may well be holding a loaded gun in mine."

There doesn't appear any major threat to this provision on the horizon other than the potential disavowal of information garnered from a search due to a laxity of specificity in the warrant's description created by inaccurate or missing wordage in the actual document. That inadvertency or insufficiency can be corrected in acquiring judicial approval for the warrant quicker and continuing instruction to law enforcement as to the scope and completeness of the warrant's detail. The improper use of the "no knock access", used most often regarding suspected drug or hostage situations must be an action constantly under scrutiny of the courts. It reflects an inadequacy of local law enforcement agencies to have the resources to be more attentive to where and how such entries will occur. A major problem appears to be the insufficient support provided the law enforcement area by the local prosecutorial officials. The answer is almost too rudimentary to speak of here, but better and more consistent communication coupled with greater trust between the agencies is the critical element.

●

The 5th Amendment

No person shall be held to answer for a capital, or otherwise infamous crime, unless on a presentment or indictment of a Grand Jury, except in cases arising in the land or naval forces, or in the Militia, when in actual service in time of War or public danger; nor shall any person be subject for the same offence to be twice put in jeopardy of life or limb; nor shall be compelled in any criminal case to be a witness against himself, nor be deprived of life, liberty, or property, without due process of law; nor shall private property be taken for public use, without just compensation.

COMMENT: For many, this is a potpourri of defense measures and tactics available to those accused to use the language of this section for their personal benefit. The Grand Jury element of due process, has to some protesting their innocence, become a claim at times of possible prosecutorial misconduct. This ageless claim often supports, some contend, that a prosecutor, with the current presentation limitations by all concerned, "can indict a ham sandwich." The defendant and or his attorney are not allowed to be present for the Grand Jury hearing or to offer testimony or facts as they relate or can provide except in certain instances allowed by the court. Technically, only the prosecution is permitted to present evidence. The argument is that such a solely singular process denies the accused the opportunity to show that the charges as they exist at the time of the requested indictment, fail to meet the challenge of reasonability and sufficiency. The greatest fear of some, particularly the families of victims or survivors of crimes against them, is that "unless the accused is convicted the first time around, the prosecution gets only one bite of the apple," concept. The legal term "double jeopardy" is automatically invoked. Simply: one chance to convict and the inability to bring the accused forward for another trial, even if after acquittal, new evidence proves the original claim of guilt was, in fact, true and provable.

Considered under English law as the principle assuring protection of incessant prosecution for the same accusation or claimed misdeed, it had been earlier practiced by the Romans. Although narrow in its application under the English jurisprudence system, it was the genesis of the American view that is so emphasized in the 5th Amendment. However, this cloak of individual freedom from ongoing prosecution can be breached in the event of jury, defense or other areas of misconduct or violation of accepted legal protocol and ethical requirements. Thus, the initial effort by the government must be sound, purposeful, and effective so as to assure a balanced and adequate approach, assuring the subsequent trial or hearing is conducted within the proscribed limits of the law.

Even those many, unfamiliar with appropriate legal commentary or verbiage, have no problem with understanding the basic premise of the much quoted and television crime drama repeated "Miranda Warning." For those not that familiar with this now famous legal requirement, it stipulates protection of anyone against self-incrimination without proper warning that such could and would be used against the individual in any later legal action. This structured admonition to any individuals arrested on suspicion of any crime became a responsibility of any arresting officer due to a U.S. Supreme Court decision, Miranda v. Arizona, 384, U.S. 436 (1966), when an Ernesto Miranda, arrested for kidnapping and armed robbery, had his conviction overturned. The ruling found he'd not been informed of his rights under the Fifth Amendment to remain silent and under the Sixth Amendment to have legal counsel even if he was not able to afford an attorney. Miranda was retried, again convicted and spent eleven years in prison. This particular incident did quantify and declare the absolute right by the accused in every situation.

More recently, in 2010, the High Court in Bergquis v. Thompson, 5560 U.S. 130 S. Ct, ruled that although the accused had the right to remain silent under questioning, and the right under the Sixth Amendment of assistance by counsel, they could waive these rights. More concisely, the right to halt questioning by law enforcement must be expressed explicitly by clear and sustainable understanding by the accused. This has led the more socially alert law enforcement agencies to also require their officers when in doubt of the accused's facility in English to assure the individual has that warning provided in their primary language. Particularly valuable in dealing with the populace in heavily ethnic minority areas.

The accused right to forestall actually testifying, is also considered by some as protection against self-incrimination and protection against a strong prosecution attempt to show inconsistencies in the defendant's statements while on the stand and under oath. Regrettably it is a right of the accused and although too often considered an essence of guilt by the legally uninformed it remains one of the basic elements of a fair hearing or trial for any individual. Protection against automatic arrest, incarceration, and denial of legal counsel and proper representation is one of the hallmarks of our judicial system. It is a set of required liberties that must never be lessened or abrogated. The "double jeopardy" prohibition aspect of this provision is paramount to a fair and equitable opportunity by the accused to receive a just hearing without fear of continuing prosecution. It should be mentioned here that although, to many, our legal system equates with justice, in this writer's opinion, that corollary is somewhat askew from the fact.

Our legal system, as enumerated in both this Amendment and all the subsequent rulings and regulations and aspects of *due process* hopefully assures each person a fair and unbiased hearing before the bar of justice at whatever level such presentations are made. As to justice itself, it will vary as to the final determination of any legal claim, prosecution or defense of an individual or action. It, viewed through such a lens, can become a rather blurred and at times, in the mind of some, a distorted perspective. In regards to the very volatile subject of the rights of defendants and the death penalty, following is a suggestion which could be assumed by some as violating the right of the defendant to life and liberty.

"That in the event double jeopardy does exist and by law must be exercised as a protection of the accused, such new information that may or could have engendered a different verdict, shall, at the earliest time reasonable, provide all and complete, such information not formerly available during the trial process to the survivors and or legal relatives of the victim(s) so they may, at their will and intent, seek legal redress against said accused or his existing or future assets, regardless of the eventual verdict."

"Furthermore, the death sentence being adjudged by a jury of the defendant's peers, and such sentence being reviewed by the next higher judicial authority and the defendant being given a period of no less than five years nor more than ten years to appeal, and such appeals having been found not warranting any further delay of the adjudged death sentence, such sentence shall be administered in the manner and at the time set forth by the governing jurisdiction having such right to proceed with said execution."

The execution by the State by any means of those adjudged of a crime to deserve this most severe of penalties has and will continue to beleaguer both liberal polemicists and those in law enforcement, and the judiciary. Adding to this controversy, the questionable production of the actual drugs to be administered and their possibility of bringing pain to the individual. To one viewpoint, it is cruel and unusual punishment. The opposition will claim the right of the people to seek like and total resolution of matters when the taking of the victim(s) lives was both heinous and deserving of the maximum penalty. The fear that legal maneuvering or a chance that the perpetrator could be released to once more commit crimes on other innocent victims drives the debate as to the viability of the death penalty. It's an emotional quagmire and the debate will continue until the High Court were to rule the implementation of the death penalty to no longer be acceptable under current law. As of now a number of states have precluded an overall court decision and themselves abolished the death penalty regardless of the crime.

Continuing discussion of the 5th Amendment, those rights referred to in the latter part are directed at the subject of "eminent domain, or the right of the local or other governing administration to take possession of land for the purpose of seeking supposed advantage to the good of the public. The ownership of said property is to be compensated in a fair and timely manner. However, in recent years, the development craze and increasing pressure on urban governments to give special consideration to removal of less income generating property so as to acquire much more tax enhancing manufacturing and retail structures has created a multitude of legal contestations. As a result, this writer feels such protection for unwarranted or improper seizure of land and low income properties has been increasingly abused in the name of community advancement. Too often, such seizure under the auspices of "eminent Domain" becomes in actuality a shadow method of transferring such private property from the original owner to another private entity. I have a suggested inclusion to possibly ameliorate this situation were it to occur.

"And that all claims for the legal insertion of `eminent domain' shall first be reviewed by selected, impartial and politically unconnected panels of those with appropriate credentials and legal authority in assessing qualitatively and by quantity the pricing available and appropriate dispensation of property as has been designated or directed as to replacement from the existing owner to the use and ownership of another party for the purposes of restoration, refurbishing, replacement, and or

removal. And that no act of dispossession shall occur to those considered physically or mentally disabled until appropriate and sufficient respite has been achieved."

•

This next Article is basic to the rights of all who face the bar of justice or become entangled within the legal system.

The 6th Amendment

In all prosecutions, the accused shall enjoy the right to a speedy and public trial by an impartial jury of the State and district wherein the crime shall have been committed, which district shall have been ascertained by law, and to be informed of the nature and cause of the accusation; to be confronted with the witnesses against him; to have compulsory process for obtaining witness in his favor, and to have the Assistance of counsel for his defense.

COMMENT: It does lend itself to the extension of trial procedure and eventual legal resolution of criminal proceedings to the degree that time becomes the most effective weapon of the defendant. It is a right that too often allows the dissolution of evidence, the eventual absence of critical forensics and witnesses, and the degrading of the right to a speedy trial as manipulated by the defense. Regrettably, although this Article refers directly to criminal matters, it is too often that such delays and procrastination in civil matters has reduced, and in many cases, almost eliminated, the petitioner's right and the law's obligation to provide speedy and prompt resolution. Here, many who approach the bar of justice, seeking satisfaction as they assume the Constitution guarantees, find themselves enmeshed in tortuous and time exaggerated legal combat.

Simply stated, this amendment assures seven specific rights enjoyed by all who enter into, whether voluntarily or by circumstance, the world of law enforcement and judicial oversight. As stipulated, it requires a speedy trial, the right to be tried in public, to be judged by an impartial jury of the defendant's peers. Additionally, to be provided sufficient information regarding the basic aspects of the charges against the accused regarding the alleged crime or misdeed. Also required, the right to confront those who would testify against the accused, and further to bring forth witnesses who would provide elements of the defensive strategy. Finally, there is the right to have an attorney represent the accused whether or not such legal counsel can be afforded.

Perhaps the most salient example of this omission from earlier law enforcement procedure was the highly publicized Gideon v. Wainwright case before the U. S. Supreme Court in early 1963. Basically it concerned a fifty-one year old white man, Clarence Earl Gideon who had been arrested for the burglary at a Panama City, FL pool hall. His crime was supposedly the damaging of a cigarette machine ant theft of money from a cash register. He appeared alone in court alone as he was too poor to afford counsel. The court transcript revealed the Judge, replying to Gideon's claim he had no lawyer and claimed his innocence, refused such appointment of an attorney stated that "under the Florida law at that time, only capital offenses require provision of defense counsel."

Sentenced to five years in prison, Gideon, personally researched and determined the Sixth Amendment and submitted a hand written appeal to the U. S. Supreme Court, actually suing the then Secretary of the Florida Corrections. Through a series of involvement by other legal persons and groups, the case was held at the High Court. The decision rendered by then Associate Justice Hugo Black unanimously in Gideon's favor. The public nature of the entire matter became subject for a popular book and later movie. Simply quantified it had a definite impact on the courts and developed the public defender system as well as the now mandated "right to counsel regardless of the type of arrest or accusation.

"This aspect of the "Miranda" statement is sometimes omitted in the flurry of search and restraint of any accused or regrettably often overtly by arresting officer(s) in order to achieve early information However it became the expected and required watchword. It is that error by law enforcement most often challenged by those claiming an accused individual was not afforded the mandatory legal advice and protection prior to any interrogation and when verified no such protection was granted creates a prosecutorial impediment to further adjudication. The required "a jury of his or her peers" brings up the inevitable question as to racial balance, gender representation and the nature of the jury participants relative to the defendant's criminal history or actual social or economic status. Can true balance in jury representation ever be achieved?

The required "speedy trial" has long been a tool for procrastination through defense measures to extend the actual appearance before a jury of his or her peer's beyond the normal limits of witness and evidence availability. The demand by some that they confront their accusers too often is the ploy to force very young children to account in court, in front of their accused molester, the hideous details of their abuse. These appearances and testimony could be held in a separate area, video confirmed, still allowing the defense to question the child out of sight of the accused but with such interrogation visually provided the accused. Thus not having to occur in the glare of cameras, strangers and particularly the accused him or herself. Might I proffer an additional bit of language?

Regardless of the public outcry when the accused might not be judicially tried sue to the required representation or reasonably speedy trial, it may be the words of U.S. Supreme Court Associate Justice, Lewis Powell, Jr. at the American Bar Association meeting speech, August 10, 1976.

"Equal justice under law is not merely a caption on the façade of the Supreme Court building, it is perhaps the most important ideal of our society. It is one of the ends for which our entire legal system exists . . . it is fundamental that justice should be the same in substance and availability, without regard to economic status."

"Such criminal prosecutions and the ability of the accused to mount a reasonably satisfactory defensive strategy shall be considered as such only within limits of time wherein both parties have been able to prove

that any delay to said trial or resolution is definitely proportional to the rights of both parties. And that readiness by one party while proceedings are delayed by continuous actions of a deleterious manner of the other party, shall be considered an attempt to thwart the efficacy of the right of either party and shall have no legal justification for further delay."

"That, in the instance where the age of the victim or a palpable witness would by the circumstance of the trial procedure itself, cause greater suffering for such victim or witness, acceptable arrangements shall be instituted to diminish or remove any such cause for the aforementioned suffering or intimidation. That seclusion of the victim from the accused, based on age and condition of the victim at the time of the trial, shall be effected and use of appropriate video transmission shall be provided all those present during the actual trial process. The defense shall have the opportunity to sufficiently question the witness or victim in such seclusion, such interrogation available to the accused via such video conferencing method.

As to the right to legal counsel, whether able to afford private representation or not, was critical to the document's authors as it spread the equality of all. However, this writer has long felt, that although judicial and legislative bodies have long been cognizant of the victim, their families and the protection of their rights, it is still the role of the judiciary to compel speedy and prompt resolution in all matters, criminal and civil.

The responsibility lies in both parties agreeing to a reasonable span of time to consummate their individual process. And then the judicial branch must recognize deficiencies in such planning and scheduling. It is the court's responsibility to assure public confidence that the rights and considerations for both sides as enumerated in this Article, are complied with faithfully and fully.

•

The 7ᵗʰ Amendment

In suits at common law, where the value in controversy shall exceed twenty dollars, the right of trial by jury shall be preserved, and no fact tried by a jury shall be otherwise re-examined in any court of the United States, than according to the rules of common law.

COMMENT: Although it is common practice for each party to waive a jury trial in common law suits and will, at times leave the interpretation of the law(s) involved, to a trial judge; the salient point of this Amendment further stipulates that in essence, no judge can substitute his opinion of any and all facts provided the jury. Nor can any appellate court invalidate a jury's decision and issue any final order on its own. It is this protection from sitting or higher judicial entities to nullify the mandate of the jury that assures interference would not become a substantive cause unless improprieties or illegal process is proven. The major problem is the exasperating and often devious postponement of such trial periods. It effectively creates an almost impossible burden on the plaintiff, thus both restricting them of a speedy resolution and the fiscal demands on their resources created by delays manufactured by the defending party. A suggested balance to this situation is hereby offered:

"That all such civil matters be required to comply with the speedy trial requirement as pertains to all such criminal cases. That each party of any such legal action provide the administering judicial authority a proposed procedure in preparing and providing all necessary and requested documents relative to the civil matter in question. That each request for delay must be attended by conclusive statements of fact as to the reason and justification for such delay. And if found to be inconclusive or without reasonable substantiation, the court shall demand immediate resolution of the matter and if such is not available after due deliberation, shall render on part of the court any final resolution and/or verdict. Furthermore,

evidence and conclusion of fact that either party has been the instigator or participant in any effort to unnecessarily delay resolution of the legal claim on the part of either party, said final verdict shall not be subject to review unless judicial misconduct or misinterpretation of the facts delivered is proven."

●

The 8th Amendment
Excessive bail shall not be required, nor excessive fines imposed, nor cruel and unusual punishments inflicted.

COMMENT: This Amendment is simple in its wordage. Yet the question of what is proper bail amount or the extent to which monetary fines or the actual incarceration level is adjudged can often create the basis for appeal. It seems that past years have brought forth numerous conflicts with the rights of the accused to what some will declare should be reasonable bail of sentences in keeping only with the nature and severity of the crime. Aside from that commentary, the 8th amendment does give the judge the prerogative of bail requirement. Considered are circumstances that must be first considered, including nature of the crime, the potential for witness and/or plaintiff intimidation and/or tampering and what is often termed "flight risk" concerning the accused. As to the assessment of fines, this aspect is too often left in the hands of the civil case juries who have, in recent years, awarded almost obscene fines and/or penalties on the party found in violation or at fault in many situations. This is particularly true in medical malpractice and injury/death suits. There needs to be a review of the conditions and potential ramifications concerning any fines or sentences or civil awards that at first examination regardless of the defendant's supposed or agreed actions some degree of moderation through insightful consideration by others with equal or greater expertise than the juries involved.

The prohibition of "cruel and unusual punishment" has been the crux of the death penalty debate. It is a lasting and volatile question but there is insufficient space herein to cover that emotional and convoluted enigma.

To the victimized, the victim's survivors, nothing but elimination of the subject of their loved one's often heinous death will satisfy the human emotion of revenge, countered by the opposition as a form of undeniable revenge. To supporters it means the impossibility of the convicted to ever repeat their crimes. Yet, there are those who feel the government has no more right to take a human life, however adjudicated or mandated in any set of laws than the individual convicted for the crime, however odious or brutal. To some, the mere incarcerating of the mass killer or unredeemable perpetrator is to allow a life of relative comfort while deserving to be removed from any opportunity to return to society via pardon or parole or commutation. This writer leaves such sensitive and inflammable considerations to others, far more able to hopefully, someday resolve a decision with which, most assuredly, not everyone will ever agree. It is a question that can never enjoy the avoidance of personal emotion.

So let us move on to what could be the basis of all Constitutional criticisms and conflict among various interpreters and exponents. The first, bears the thrust of many groups as to more recent attempts by local, state, and national legislatures to engage in formation of laws that are felt to be in denial of the people's right to determine direction or substance of such laws or constitutional interpretations. It has been reinterpreted many times over the years. Little referred to by students of the Constitution or those supposed legal experts of that document, it was a proposed barrier to elected officials attempting a much greater control over the intents of the Constitution than existed. It has, during the past numerous decades, still been bombarded by social activists and liberal interventionists to allow increased domination by vested interest regardless of any aspect of the Constitution's original design.

•

The 9th Amendment

The enumeration in the constitution of certain rights shall not be construed to deny or disparage others retained by the people.

COMMENT: Here is the first caveat to the whole of the document. A position by the writers of the Constitution as to protection of the assembly of citizenry to any overt or inadvertent attempt by their elected representatives to alter in any form, the original dictates of the document as to personal freedoms. It requires a total legislative review, majority vote to submit to the people and construction of an amendment that could or should mitigate the proposed conflict or clarify what was formerly contended as requiring a more current interpretation. It will always be the thorn in the side of those who feel the Constitution is a flexible tool to be utilized as they wish, depending on current influence and political control.

●

The 10th Amendment

The powers not delegated to the United States by the Constitution nor prohibited by it to the States, are reserved to the States respectively, or to the people.

COMMENT: Here we confront the most contentious aspect of our current national administration. One that has occurred numerous times in the past, but more recently has become the lightening rod that has polarized the ability of the three branches of government to function with any degree of affable compromise. This article directs attention to the limitations on the right of legislatures and the scope of their elected authority to tinker with the basic format of the Constitution. It was expected by the authors of the Constitution that no effort was needed to further explain or detail the process reserving powers not delegated to Congress or specifically to the States. It remained so obvious that it became a covenant between the legislator and the people. However, there arose this continuing battle between the wording of both the Ninth and Tenth Amendment and those desiring to expand the federal power concept. It has been argued that neither Amendment seeks to be a limitation on recognized and agreed federal powers, but rather, a safeguard against unfettered change to the Constitution that can and would decrease personal liberties as enfranchised in the bulk of the document.

Our government was structured by allocation of specific powers to each of the three branches; the Executive Office, the Congressional and the Judicial. Conflict over division of these powers has continued since the early days of our country. Intruding into this struggle is the growing involvement of the Supreme Court into the qualitative refitting of existing law through their opinions, considered the final say in any legal question.

In recent years certain national administrations, either through their compliant legislatures or executive order, have sought to minimize what is normally referred to as "States rights". It is an action and political aim by some that has caused conflict and was the genesis of those events leading to the tragedy of the Civil War. The states are the representation of the original thirteen colonies. The strongly worded dialogue that encompassed the initial constitutional considerations in the late 1780s carries forth today. A federal government that has total control over the particular nature of any individual state portends a domination too similar to that which our forefathers fought to deny the English King. It is a component of the Constitution that must never be denied or obviated. I would suggest the following application of personal and State's rights as refers to those posers who insist they have powers constitutionally belonging to them and not to Congress nor the Executive Branch.

"When disagreement and obvious conflict between those proposals and/or submitted legal challenges to such rights shall occur, it shall require no less than two-thirds vote of the Congress with written acceptance of the President and concurrence of the Supreme Court for the decision as to who shall supersede the other in enactment and implementation of such proposal or law, prior to final resolution of such matters. And that all such debate or hearings, including those of the Congress, any designated or assumed committees and that of the Supreme Court, shall be both publicized and made available through whatever print and or broadcast medium is in use at that time so as to widely and sufficiently inform all interested parties and the general public."

To assure that the powers of the national government not exceed the value of their effect on the individual rights of the citizenry, this amendment must become the rule of law regarding this relationship between states and the national government. Without such control and strict adherence to this prohibition, national legislators can become ersatz controllers of freedoms assured the individual and thus violate the purpose of these two amendments meant to provide the individual states their right to administer their citizens in a manner they feel most propitious.

•

The 11th Amendment

The Judicial power of the United States shall not be construed to extend to any suit or law or equity, commenced or prosecuted against one of the United States by Citizens of another State or by Citizens or Subjects of any Foreign State.

RATIFICATION: Feb. 7, 1795

COMMENT: This has become the vehicle that the Federal government was able to utilize to finally eliminate the vicious, illegal and racially blinded refusal of southern state's courts to indict or convict those accused and in many cases, evidently guilty of violence against African Americans and others of ethnic or ideological differences. The right of removal of such cases, long disparaged or disregarded as to timely and sufficient resolution, referring to the racial imbalance of the late 19th Century through more than half of the 20th Century, is one of the changes in the original legal standing of all citizens to come out of that tremulous nature of the judicial system in the south. Yet, it is this almost total immunity by local, state and federal government from being the respondent in any legal action. There are exceptions and allowances too numerous and somewhat convoluted to discuss here. Nonetheless, any government, at whatever level, can position itself as a Minotaur of resistance when the individual citizen or group decides to litigate, whatever the cause or reason. It is suggested that an additional caveat be considered.

"That furthermore, it shall be the right and where imminent injustice or failure of the local and or state judiciary to act because of the insufficiency or laxity of the prosecutorial aspect to act promptly, to assume insertion of non-locally allied prosecutorial and judicial resources to assure the rights being threatened or delayed shall be resolved in a timely and acceptable manner."

The current malaise within our congressional structure and the near inane behavior of our elected representatives has brought greater attention to this next amendment, the system for electing the President and Vice President of the United States. During the past twelve or so years, two major controversies have arisen regarding how the electorate's vote would be counted. The method for determining the necessary majority of votes for one or more candidates has nearly brought this nation to its philosophical knees with the highly disputed Bush/Gore election fiasco. This was followed by the later Bush/Kerry debacle which did little to stem the growing tide against the "Electoral College" process as enumerated in Article XII. We first need to again review this rather nebulous intention of the amendment's writers.

•

The 12th Amendment

The Electors shall meet in their respective states and vote by ballot for President and vice-President, one of whom, at least, shall, shall not be an inhabitant of the same state with themselves; they shall name in their ballots the person voted for as President, and in distinct ballots the person voted for as vice-President, and they shall make distinct lists of all persons voted for as President, and all persons voted for as Vice-President, and of the votes for each, which lists they shall sign and certify, and transmit sealed to the seat of the government of the United

States, directed to the President of the Senate; - the President of the Senate , shall in the presence of the Senate and House of Representatives, open all the certificates and the votes shall then be counted; The person having the greatest number of votes for President, shall be the President, if number be a majority of the whole number of Electors appointed; and if no person have such majority, then from the persons having the highest numbers not exceeding three on the list of those voted for as President, the House of Representatives shall choose immediately, by ballot, the President. But in choosing the President, the votes shall be taken by states, the representation from each state having one vote; a quorum for this purpose shall consist of a member or members from two-thirds of the states, and a majority of all the states shall be necessary to a choice. The person having the greatest number of votes as Vice-President, shall be the Vice-President, if such number be a majority of the whole number of Electors appointed, and if no person have a majority, then from the two highest numbers on the list, the Senate shall choose the Vice-President; a quorum for the purpose shall consist of two-thirds of the whole number of Senators, and a majority of the whole number shall be necessary to a choice. But no person constitutionally ineligible to the office of President shall be eligible to that of Vice-President of the United States." and House.

RATIFICATION: Jun 15, 1804

COMMENT: Within its wordage is a conflicting inconsistency, further complicating the use of the term 'electors' individually to select the next Chief Executive. There always exists frustration by the citizenry that although they all individually have cast their vote, it was actually the 'electors' who control who wins and who loses. "One man, one vote" has been the mantra of the personal liberty advocates. The right of the individual to dictate his or her preference of who shall lead their country for the next four years has been the mainstay of most Constitutionalists. However, a twit from one of our more southern regions, once commented, 'That ain't what it really is'. So let us consider what was in the minds of the framers of the Constitution and its later amendments when this expected result of the right to vote was first enumerated.

From the beginning, our Founding Fathers were concerned that the fate of the newly formed democracy never fall to the whims of those they and society had for centuries not felt competent to direct the fortunes of government. This categorization of society was ingrained so deeply that it permeated every attempt to provide freedoms that for millennia had been denied the common man. To the more educated and often landed gentry of the mid-18th Century, it was assumed one required a degree of intellect, sufficient schooling, and a position that engendered respect from his associates to accomplish such complex and sophisticated process to be capable of definitive leadership roles. As was the traditional societal belief then, the opposite gender was not mentioned anywhere within the Constitution until the 19th Amendment almost one hundred and forty years later. Thus, the document remained a male oriented construction. Yet, aside from that aspect, peculiar to its time, the question still exists as to why does every citizen's vote not count fully when the directed procedure of the Twelfth Amendment is consistently enacted each quadrennial election period?

What then do the proponents of one eligible citizen, one eligible vote demand? That the President of the United States be elected by a majority of the votes cast. It seems a simple and rather clear declaration of purpose and meaning. However, we need to also look at the obverse side of this testy question. When surveying where and in what numbers lie the major centers of potential voters, one needs only consider, the greater New York area, Los Angeles basin, the major cities of the Southwest, Houston, Dallas and San Antonio. Not to forget Chicago, the Philadelphia complex, south to Atlanta and the ever burgeoning southern Florida peninsula. With the electoral system, the major candidates for national office need only concentrate on those states with the largest number of electoral votes. Control them and the other, less populated areas are relatively unimportant, say the critics of the process dictated in the Twelfth Amendment.

Currently there are 538 electoral votes based on the population of which 270 are required to gain the Presidency. Mathematically, only 15 states now have the electoral votes to reach that goal. Thus, why not concentrate only on those states. Why waste time and funds meandering throughout those much less dominant electoral sites such as Montana, Wyoming, Utah, and the Dakotas, the broad vastness of the Midwest and on and on. Thus, approximately thirty-five of the fifty states could very easily be totally excised from the presidential selection. Even with a minimal majority, say, 50.1% in each state, a candidate could win the election although the popular vote could be far in favor of the candidate's principal opponent. But the new census could change that somewhat, yet still not altering this formula for acquiring the necessary electoral level required.

Let us consider the alternative, the singular concept that every eligible vote be counted and the candidate receiving the majority of those votes becomes the winner. Now that the official 2010 Census has been completed, the laborious process of being tabulated into its many subsections and categories has seemed to change the political representation picture very little other than the rising political position of several minorities, African-American and Latino. What it will also show is that our country has reached appreciably over 300 million population. That does not include what could be a reported over eleven million illegal entries to this country, undocumented and thus, probably uncounted.

The inability of the supposed popular vote to measure the election results, is what the opponents of the Electoral College system declare violates the one man, one vote concept. To them, that is the bastion of the right of all to select who shall represent them in the Executive Mansion. So let us research the mathematics of that presumption. We will use sixteen of the fifty states as the template; California, Florida, Texas, Ohio, Massachusetts, Georgia, Illinois, Indiana, Michigan, Missouri, New

Jersey, New York, North Carolina, Pennsylvania, Virginia and Washington. At the time of this writing, US Census bureau qualified estimates places the total population of these states at approximately two hundred and three million people. Again this does not count the undocumented aliens and illegal entries. That equates in total to sixty-six percent of the total national population. Coupled with that is the further calculation of electoral votes which for these sixteen states is three hundred and twenty nine at present levels. To be even more rigid in our counting, let's eliminate the three states that only account for thirty-four votes. That reduces the total to two hundred and ninety five votes. With the winning number set at two hundred and seventy, surely one can again see the merit and financially sound practice of concentrating on these states, leaving the remainder virtually without any influence on the national candidacy of whoever is the candidate of choice for them.

So what direction should we take? The Electoral College and the popular voice are still dependent on these sixteen states unless the popular vote can be distributed more equally among all the states. Yet, both approaches favor the candidate with the political and campaign machine, the funding, and the ability to capture ongoing prominence in all the media reports and coverage. Without the ability of the less populated states to gain some type of measurable parity with the major urban centers, the question of which is the fairest system remains moot. Where once minorities were considered a relatively lesser effect on past elections, today, ethnicity has become the tipping factor in many local, state, and national campaign efforts.

It is projected that currently the African-American share of the total population has reached approximately fourteen percent. The Hispanic-Latino share now reflects fifteen percent or more of the total number. Added to this is the projected five percent Asian influx as well as other smaller non-Caucasian groups, when gathered with the rest, will soon equal approximately forty percent of the total population. This is the core of the non-traditional voting block all future campaigns will target at most legislative election levels. The political machine that can dominate this specialized categorization, can potentially control election outcomes for many years to come. And in doing so, could create a domination of the public interest and welfare never desired by our Founding Fathers.

What is the answer? Only time will tell. Population changes continue to affect the electoral vote count every four years. Until then, it will be the responsibility of the campaigner and his or her supporters to recognize that to win, one needs to control the power centers, both through total population being courted and the rising influence of the ethnicity that has become a governing factor in many areas of our country. We would suggest, for purposes of greater examination of the validity of the present system of the effect, that the two methods of presidential election results be tabulated on a continuing basis to either substantiate or minimize the contention that the current method of presidential selection be revised or discontinued. It would undoubtedly become a testy paradigm of conflicting opinions as to how the voter's voice is to be heard and recorded. The following is offered:

"And in addition to the process as encompassed in this article, it is hereby required that the delineation and computation of voter balance and effect of total votes cast on the result of any national election of the President of the United States, shall be reviewed each and every ten years. And such indications of voter concerns as to the efficacy of the result shall become a matter of direct concern of both Houses of Congress. Thus any reasonable attempt to rectify and determine insufficiency or inequality shall be considered and where applicable or viable under the law can and shall be put to the eligible voting populace as could or would be changed or modified through a legally and acceptable process of a proposed amendment.

●

The 13th Amendment

Section 1. Neither slavery nor involuntary servitude, except as punishment for crime whereof the party shall have been duly convicted, shall exist within the United States, or any place subject to their jurisdiction.

Section 2. Congress shall have power to enforce this article by appropriate legislation.

RATIFICATION: Dec. 6, 1865

COMMENT: This is a simple declaration outlawing a sin of our fathers perpetuated well before the beginning of our nation and during its formative days in the late 17th Century. It was the staple of the economy of peoples since before the time of Abraham and the Pharaohs. Still, it is an abomination that has existed throughout millennium from the earliest recorded days of mankind's relatively civilized society. However, there still exists a form of system of economic bondage, most evident in the near serf like conditions in certain areas of our agricultural and materials manufacturing and processing operations.

Yet, what in 1861 was considered by one side as the principle of states' rights and by the opposition as a need to halt the potential dissolution of the union, soon became a conflict that was in reality the struggle to erase the stain of slavery from a nation yet to have celebrated its 80th birthday as a the most unique creation of government ever seen. A conflict in which over 600,000 Americans would die – both southern and northern.

The traditional "stoop labor" endured by many minorities from Hispanic-Latino groups can easily be considered servitude. Coupled with the thousands of European immigrants who during the latter part of the 19th Century and into the 20th were subjugated to harsh working conditions for barely survival wages marked enslavement of many workers to a system that fortunately has bettered over the years. But what is part of what have been called "sweat shops", still prevalent in parts of the New York textile industry. Yet, with this Constitutional declaration that followed the Lincoln issued Emancipation Proclamation of 1863 by two years, there arose no direct line from the enslavement of some to the total equality of all. The Civil War saw the loss of 625,000 Americans on both sides of the conflict – two percent of the then total population.

As the writer, allow me to present a brief sidebar to this subject. For years, since this amendment, certain groups have used the history of slavery in our country as a pedantic crusade. We have been forced to endure the vitriolic semantics of a number of self-endowed civil rights activists. Too often their venal personal interests have overshadowed the greatness of many true advocates of the demand that color, race, gender or social proclivity should not deny any member of the American community full and equal rights in the field of economics, before the bar of justice, and within the entire social structure. These sycophantic sophists are well known. Unfortunately, the media and a recent national administration has allowed several of these mental miscreants far too much public acclaim. Such individuals do more harm than the good they proclaim as their mission. Their cacophony of callous disregard of the truth or reason has too often dimmed the voice of such true leaders as Martin Luther King, Jr. and others, who had continually preached non-violence and prudent, rational response to contended offenses against their fellow minorities, and other lesser advantaged members of society.

When Plessey v. Ferguson, 163 U.S. 537 (1896), ostensibly legitimized racial segregation even though technically retaining most of the basic rights intended in the earlier Emancipation Proclamation, it was a shallow attempt to satiate the southern elements of the dominant Democratic Party. It did little to overcome the prejudice that was the menu of freedom dictated by many of the southern states dominated white power structure.

Their continual clamoring and excessive reference to the regretted days of servitude by these carrion of convolution do more harm than good in advancing the cause of equality many have suffered and even died to eliminate over the years. Lest these pseudo social scientists forget, slavery was an objectionable but accepted form of commerce not only by our early citizenry but was imbued in the people we came from and the societies many others supported. Can slavery ever be totally abolished throughout the world – doubtful, as it is too germane and critical to the wealth acquisition of too many other societies?

To the south, it was considered an economic necessity brought on by their lack of industrial facility. This however did not and still does not, in any fashion, countenance or excuse this horrible blemish on our early history. Thus, we need to expend our energy more to assure no one within our dominion is ever forced into any type of domination that could be or might become a form of slavery. Possibly the following might clarify what has become a continuation, if not in name, at least in operational practice of the original abomination.

Today the abomination of slavery in our early history is bandied about by those with little or no understanding of the conditions of economic survival at that time. Not intending to justify this abhorrent practice, modern ardent activists for total equality in every facet of social existence have abused the process of rational protest by continually referring to a time and situation they neither understand nor have any qualitative or quantitative knowledge to effectively discuss regarding its evolution. As a result their constant haranguing, and at times violence-impacted public protestations have seriously damaged a cogent and nationally subscribed discussion of why we must achieve the racial parity long demanded.

"That any act of servitude through demands for illegal activity, excessive labor requirement, insufficient or legally impermissible wages or any conditions placing the individual or group used or employed under duress, suffering or incapacity to receive benefits due any and all workers, regardless of present status in the country, shall be considered a violation of this Amendment and subject to those regulations and penalties for such violations, whether overt or inadvertent."

This next article was initially proposed by Congressional resolution in 1866 eventually being ratified in July, 1968. Long in the forefront of both the legal right to hold elective office and the growing concern over immigration, particularly from the Southern portion of this hemisphere, it has engendered lengthy commentary and, at times, rather heated discussion.

•

The 14th Amendment

Section 1 - All persons born or naturalized in the United States, and subject to the jurisdiction thereof, are citizens of the United States and of the State wherein they reside. No State shall make or enforce any law which shall abridge the privileges or immunities of citizens of the United States; nor shall any State deprive any person of life, liberty or property without due process of law; nor deny to any person within its jurisdiction the equal protection of the laws.

RATIFICATION: July 9, 1868

COMMENT: The 14th Amendment not only made the black person a citizen of the country but also of the state wherein he or she resided. This became one of the thorniest issues in the post-Civil War era and its subsequent Reconstruction Period. The definition of the criteria or rather any prohibitions against election to the offices specified in this article, have little changed over the years since its writing.

Racism is a part of the social dogma taught or learned by association in those areas where the struggle for equality poses a threat to the mainstream Caucasian power structure. Regrettably, the principal black, or more politically correct nomenclature, African-American organizations, continue to use charges of racism and discrimination to voice their claxon calls for equality in advantage and opportunity, at times in excess of the actual substance of the word. No one doubts the need to continually refine and conduct with strength, all rules and administrative processes that will assure such equality in the work place, the political structure, legislative representation, and all social services.

Additionally, it opened the way for the matter of sexual discrimination and bias to become a salient issue for years to come. The resulting case law and various litigations have and will cover an extensive spectrum of such gender discriminatory actions, whether benign or overt.

This aspect of the 14th Amendment grant of due process is far too extensive and at times, too complicated to discuss herein, other than to say, the controversy of sexual equality and the balance of the genders as to equal rights and privileges will continue well beyond this writer's term.

The Constitution speaks to the right of all to be free without prejudice because of sex, race, religion, and other distinguishable variances. It cannot, however, totally change a societal attitude that was too deeply engrained from years before. At least not immediately. With the inclusion of the great number of minorities incarcerated in our prisons, this deeply felt bias is even more difficult to lessen, much less fully eliminate. Again, this writer must leave such paramount considerations to the effort of the masses to correct and it must be corrected.

Another aspect of individual's rights as stated within the 14th Amendment, is the expanding influx of illegal persons from the countries south of our borders. The practice of pregnant women striving to cross the U.S. border, either illegally or via normal tourist or guest documentation is fraught with difficulties for all persons and entities. When their child is born, the inevitable question is asked. Does the 14th Amendment automatically grant that newborn American citizenship? In addition, through the resulting claim, will it allow the mother to also remain without consequences? This highly sensitive and volatile subject has brought to the attention of numerous liberal organizations a new cause. Their intent has been to severely criticize any local, state or federal authority who refuse the progressivist demands that undocumented immigrants should be immediately granted all freedoms and benefits earned by others who are or have procedurally become citizens. Furthermore, it is requested that these mothers and their children be provided a much speedier path to citizenship not available to many other applicants over the years.

Additionally the world is now faced with a massive infusion of peoples fleeing the ongoing violence in the Middle East. Searching for both protection from raging conflicts, many also are seeking more than the barely subsistence existence the constant warfare has forced them to endure. The question is, where and how can they be both safe and achieve a semblance of emotional and societal balance. Who and where would they be reasonably accommodated, has become the pressing concern as economic, cultural, and religious circumstances have caused increased political upheaval and public resistance in many instances.

As an aside, what of the unique status some individuals enjoy of having dual citizenship? Which jurisdiction has dominance in matters involving accusations of illegal or ethical violations of the laws of one country as opposed to that of the other? When the two countries are at odds as to pursuing legal action for such contended offenses, how and by whom should the ultimate decision be rendered?

It had long been considered a prime responsibility of the federal government to protect the borders of this country from invasion, illegal or unauthorized incursion, or transit by undocumented individuals or materials. Instead, we are faced with the contested balance of power between the individual states that border our neighbor to the south and other states as well and the government itself. The question appears to this writer as rather simple. We either fulfill the commitment of national security promised to the general public or incur increasing financial burden and potential aggregation of criminal elements through lax or insufficient surety at our borders. It is a conundrum that can only be resolved through conscientious and fully bipartisan effort by all elected officials. This requires the tempering of the ultra-leftist attitude that everyone who, by legal or illegal means, enters this country should immediately become a recipient of all our nation can offer.

It must be emphasized that the limitations imposed by the Constitution on actions of the governments, both state and federal, are indispensable in preserving both public and private rights. By enforcing these limitations through the judicial process, self-governing communities can effectively protect the rights of their individual constituencies and minorities as a whole. The "Liberty", as guaranteed in the due process clause meant, in the early years of our country, almost definitively to include liberty of contracts as well as liberty to include personal, social, and political rights and privileges. However, more recently, this liberty is too often espoused at a total denial of any restrictions and a total prerogative to control any situation without consideration of opposing or affected parties or conditions of use.

Section 2. Representatives shall be apportioned among the several States according to their respective numbers, counting the whole number of persons in each state, excluding Indians not taxed. But when the right to vote in any election for the choice of electors for President and Vice President of the United States, Representatives in congress, the Executive and Judicial officers of a State, or the members of the legislature thereof is denied to any of the male inhabitants of such State, being twenty-one years of age and citizens of the United States, or in any way abridged, except for participation in rebellion, or other crime, the basis of representation therein shall be reduced in the proportion which the number of such male citizens shall bear to the whole number of male citizens twenty-one years of age in any State.

COMMENT: The national census every ten years, controls the ratio of representation in the House to the then determined population of each state. If the census is controlled and accurate, it is a fair way to adequately provide true proportional representation. However, with the massive influx of illegal or undocumented individuals, there is always the fear that representation will be developed from a mountain of incorrect or insufficiently compiled population data. The sensitivity of who should have the right to vote is one of the most conscious concerns of every American. Validity and correctness of that process must never be allowed improper or biased interpretation or implementation.

Section 3. No person shall be a Senator or Representative in congress or elector of the President or Vice-President, or hold any office, civil or military, under the United States or any State, who having previously taken an oath as a member of Congress, or as an officer of the United States, or as a member of any State legislature, or as an executive or judicial officer of any State, to support the Constitution of the United States, shall have engaged in insurrection or rebellion against the same, or given aid or comfort to the enemies thereof. But Congress may by a vote of two-thirds of each House, remove such disability.

Section 4. The validity of the public debt of the United States, authorized by law, including debts incurred for payment of pensions and bounties for services in suppressing insurrection or rebellion, shall not be questioned. But neither the United States nor any State, shall assume or pay any debt or obligation incurred in aid of insurrection or rebellion against the United States, or any claim for the loss or emancipation of any slave; but all such debts, obligations and claims shall be held illegal and void.

Section 5. The congress shall have the power to enforce, by appropriate legislations, the provisions of this Article.

COMMENT: The language is somewhat convoluted but the reader must remember it was not only the original concept of providing certain expected liberties, but in the language of a period when less media and ersatz experts were present to supposedly define each and every expression or word usage. Section 3 particularly referred to those who had served on the opposite side during the Civil War, including Robert E. Lee, Jefferson Davis and a number of other less notables who participated in that conflict. However, on Christmas Day, 1869, President Andrew Johnson issued a total amnesty for all who had been involved with the southern cause, thus ending that specific restriction. The minimization of the rights of American Indians, not then considered citizens, has since been rectified but still retains the scars of a prejudice against the "original residents" of our country.

However, the "anchor baby" term, denoting the ability of illegal entry by non-citizens to acquire citizenship for their offspring born after that illegal entry, has become the proverbial burr under the conservative saddle. Opponents contend this is merely a method to legitimize an otherwise unlawful act. They further state that the pressure to provide their children with citizenship has increased the continuing compulsion of many to make the hazardous journey across our southern borders or any of our borders, really. It is their latest position that this particular language in this Amendment was strictly to assure the newly freed slaves at the end of the Civil War not be disenfranchised after the slaughter of so many to achieve their freedom.

And further, to make certain former slave states did not actuate laws to deprive them of those rights of citizenship. So, the current use of that part of the Amendment is not valid in allowing or promoting the right of illegal entries to use this as their right to offspring citizenship. In this writer's opinion, it was not the intent of the eventual supporters of this amendment that it should become an operative codicil to the basic intent solely to free the black man and in its ratification to bring the southern supporters back into full citizenship.

More so, critics complain, such a birthright has further clogged our lower education grades with a growing number of children who have little or no English language capability, thus burdening an already overloaded and dysfunctional education system. Opponents to this rule are adamant that to continue allowing this access potential, creates publicly emotional outcries when illegal parents are being slated for deportation but their children can remain as they are, by virtue of the application of the 14th Amendment, citizens of this country.

Supporters of this section of the 14th Amendment insist it is an engraved rule of the Constitution and cannot be changed without a concurring vote by a majority of states as dictated in the law itself.

Section 2 is the governing rule wherein the membership in the House of Representatives is continually being reviewed with each decade and reapportioned based on rise or decrease in population. It was as fair as any creation of a human precept can be in those convoluted times. If however, the representation of each state were to remain stagnant, an imbalance of citizen participation would be materially affected. Regrettably, a change in population, the movement from the rural to the urban areas, the desire to seek the sun and leave the colder climes, has also too often deprived many of their direct voice in the lower house.

Section 3 – Dictates the requirements prohibiting prior acts of insurrection or rebellion, and was designed for a time when what was to be still retained could be the possible loyalties of the former monarchial control. It is somewhat antiquated in today's modern interpretation of what has long before passed, but should remain if only as an integral reference to the Constitution's evolvement through its lifetime.

Section 4 – It has only been the recent controversy and juvenile bickering over how much or when or if the national debt ceiling should ever occur, that this part of the Amendment was ever raised to public consciousness. There are those on both sides of the legislative aisle who claim the President, under the auspices of this article, could order a raise in the national debt ceiling. Which would again create continuing turmoil in the legislative process.

When considering the various elements of this Amendment it is important to remember the comment of Associate Justice Brewer in Budd v. New York when he declared, "The paternal theory of government is to me odious. The utmost possible liberty to the individual, and the fullest possible protection to him and his property is both the limitation and duty of government."

•

The 15th Amendment

Section 1. The right of the citizens of the United States to vote shall not be denied or abridged by the United States or by any State on account of race, color, or previous condition of servitude.

Section 2. The Congress shall have the power to enforce this Article by appropriate legislation.

RATIFICATION: Feb. 3, 1870

COMMENT: Here exists in a few sentences the freedom that many fought in the Civil War to obtain and perpetuate for the black man during the contentious period of the late 19th and first half of the 20th Century over the right of state sovereignty to decide, slave or free. Although bastardized in its interpretation and implementation by a number of southern states for the better part of a hundred years, it became the ensign of the later civil rights movement. Oddly omitted from most political campaign rhetoric is the fact that although the Emancipation Proclamation emanated from the first Republican party president, Abraham Lincoln, and the initial Reconstruction was begun under his Republican Vice President, Andrew Johnson, the savagery against blacks for the rest of the 19th and a large part of the 20th Century, occurred in states controlled by Democratic administrations.

This is not intended to place total blame on any one political group during that period. There were times when the opposition party was in power and could have enacted legislation and taken much stronger legal means to lessen the inequality that so often ran rampant both in the southern states and other areas. Still it enflames the rhetoric on both sides of the continuing civil rights dialogue. However, it must be noted the 15th Amendments proposed to provide voting rights to those initially referred to in the 14th Amendment for consideration by the states, received initial overwhelming support of the more radical Republican members of Congress. It was grudgingly approved by the Democratic members as a method to achieve greater political posture after the end of the Civil War. However they feared the amendment would create thousands of new voters endeared to the Republican Party. Surprisingly it was eventually some northern Republican industrialists who feared that the predominant number of now liberated African Americans would be dominated by a Democratic controlled south where the Ku Klux Klan aided with their terrorist actions the development of the infamous controlling "Jim Crow laws" and conditions. Ironically it was the State of Georgia that cast the ultimate final vote for approval.

•

The 16th Amendment

The Congress shall have the power to lay and collect taxes on incomes, from whatever source derived, without apportionment among the several States and without regard to any census or enumeration.

RATIFICATION: Feb. 3, 1913

COMMENT: Each April fifteenth, most Americans recognize the federal government's right to assess and collect taxes but fret over what has become the increasingly obese tome known as the Federal Income Tax Regulations. A publication that burdens to exasperation even the most proficient expert of the regulations and conditions contained therein. Every quadrennial election period, declarations are forthcoming from presidential and congressional applicants swearing to see to the simplification of a tax code that has become the butt of jokes and bane of every American. Sad to say, that will never be the case.

An interesting side note regarding the legitimacy of enacting of the 16th Amendment, and thus the creation of an Income tax format, was a primary element in the fictional work, "Patriot Threat" by well-known author Steve Berry (St. Martin's Publishing Group, copyright 2015). In his book, Berry describes the contestation of the Amendment by a number of groups contending the actual amendment is not in reality a part of the Constitution as ratified inasmuch as the document contained minor textual errors. E.g. "income" instead of "incomes." Also, the word "remuneration" instead of "enumeration," plus several other rather indistinct variances to the originally intended text, its opponents claiming that made the amendment invalid. Proposed by President Theodore Roosevelt in 1909, it was ratified in 1913 by a measurably large vote in both houses.

Regardless of all the attempts to disavow the 16th Amendment, Supreme Court decisions; Field v. Clark, 143 U.S. 649 (1892) and Leser v. Garnett, 258 U.S. 130 (1922) definitely directed that the function of a state legislature to pass on a proposed amendment is not subject to individual actions by people of the state attempting to limit its eventual ratification. Both tended to refer to "non-delegation doctrine", pointing to the understanding that Congress has the legislative power to enact amendments through the constitutionally applied procedure and that seemed to end that particular controversy. It was in 1943 when President Franklin Roosevelt enabled a firmer collection of income tax by decreeing its withdrawal from wages and salaries before being submitted to its recipients. That may have become the instant desire for antacids and other gastrointestinal relief.

However, here is a suggested addition to this article that could at least demand attention by the Legislatures and government minions and their required public defense of all new inclusions and/or changes in existing regulations. If not more fully abridged, the current tax code needs measurable editing. Here is a possible suggestion.

"That no more than every three years, Congress and those commissioned to lead by direction or committee position, shall entertain and implement public hearings whose main purpose shall be the following; (a) A clear explanation in writing of any revised tax regulations that have created either more inexact meaning to an existing or proposed changed or increased specific required payment levels.

(b) That such hearings shall be available on the Internet or public broadcasting, well publicized in advanced and for which transcripts can and shall be made available through the government printing office at a cost proven to just cover the actual production of such printing. Or the details of all such hearings shall be made available on the Internet for downloading by citizens and organizations at no additional cost.

And when in conflict with those stated intents by any member of Congress as to the need to make adjustments and/or reverse said proposed regulations, such shall be heard on the floor of Congress and moved to vote without prohibition or delay by any existing or designated committee assigned to supervise tax regulatory process and administration. Furthermore, that all such proposed changes in the tax law that shall materially alter or revise prior regulations and as considered by opponents to be in disfavor to the citizenry, shall be held for implementation until all discussion and review is completed."

That theoretical "eight hundred pound gorilla" that lurks behind each tax preparation is nominally the Federal Internal Revenue Service – the IRS. It is agreed the federal government has and should have the right to levy taxes. What is needed, in this writer's opinion, is a method where the voice of the people and conscientious and informed dissent can be presented and publicly heard to uncover any disproportionate use of powers by the IRS mechanism that is not permitted by a strict interpretation of the Constitution. We must use the Constitutional power given the citizen to seek redress against offenses or behavior considered ill taken or administered.

●

The 17ᵗʰ Amendment

The Senate of the United States shall be composed of two Senators from each State, elected by the people thereof for six years; and each Senator shall have one vote. The electors in each State shall have the qualifications requisite for electors of the most numerous branch of the State legislatures.

When vacancies happen in the representation of the State in the Senate, the executive authority of such State shall issue writs of election to fill such vacancies: Provided, that the legislature of any State may empower the executive thereof to make temporary appointments until the people fill the vacancies by election as the legislature may direct.

The Amendment shall not be so construed as to affect the election or term of any Senator chosen before it becomes valid as part of the Constitution.

RATIFICATION: April 8, 1913

COMMENT: These few words seem very simple in form and probably intent. Yet, over the years, the particular group in power has too often debased the premise of fair representation. This varies to the degree it has become another political grab bag, depending on the level of conflict between the two major political parties in any particular state. I would suggest possible inclusion of the following addition or legislated interpretation:

"Furthermore, that the right of the eligible citizens in the state to be assured their vote will be permitted, such election must be held within a space of no more than three months after such vacancy should occur. And that the State legislature involved, shall not be permitted to effect any rule of ascendancy or replacement that shall alter materially, bias the process, or diminish the right of the eligible constituency to exercise their right to validate any such accession to the vacated office through their uninhibited vote."

Here again this writer will forward an opinion he has held for years. That the current redundancy of membership and lifelong control of individual representational positions must end. I am a firm believer in term limits for both Houses of Congress. Serving in Congress is an honor and a public service and not a career. Our Founding Fathers envisioned citizen legislators, not long term job seekers. It was not to be an objective where annual reimbursements in lieu of any other type of work effort become an extended stay at the tax payer's expense. I suggest the following as one or a number of approaches that might be conjured:

"That those attaining the office of Senator shall be allowed to hold said position for no more than two-six year terms. At the end of which, said position holder shall be restrained from running for said position for no less than four years or to be appointed to replace any such open position during that four-year hiatus. And during that period, shall not be

permitted to serve in any paid or consultative position within the federal government or receive and accept any ambassadorial position during said period. Nor shall said individual be permitted to hold the position of membership in the House of Representatives during that hiatus. The single exception, these limitations shall not refer to nomination and/or appointment to the United States Supreme Court."

"After the end of the aforesaid four-year period, said individual may again apply for and campaign for that or like position with the understanding that the same three term conditions, as were contingent to the individual's former membership, including those limitations in reference to the House of Representatives as shall be further described herein, shall remain in effect."

"That no member of the House of Representatives shall serve more than five-two year terms at which time said individual shall remain out of elected office to that position or the Senate of the United States for a period of no less than four years. And those conditions appertaining to membership in the United States Senate regarding interim appointments or consultative positions shall also apply to the House of Representatives."

The lifelong careers of Senators and Representatives often exceed thirty to forty years, breeding insufficiency of fresh thought. It becomes a tax supported career, often far in excess, if not totally eclipsing any prior work function that could have prepared said individuals for a more balanced view of their constituents needs. Our Founding Fathers felt strongly that representing a constituency was a privilege. That it was an act of selfless public service. It was not to be a method of supping at the public trough to the detriment of other viable candidates. The framework of our ship of state rusts when we allow it to be moored and never taken out into the seas of potentially fresh viewpoint and divergent opinions, which can benefit the good of the country. This dominance in retaining one's seat in either house, has challenged the potential for opportunity by others to apply, campaign, and potentially gain Congressional membership. Such lack of opportunity has created in the minds of many, stagnation of fresher viewpoint or application of greater constituency participation. It can possibly create a pseudo aristocracy in conflict with the intent of the Founding Fathers.

•

The 18th Amendment

Section 1. – After one year from the ratification of this article the manufacture, sale, or transportation of intoxicating liquors within, the importation thereof into, or the exportation thereof from the United States and all territory subject to the jurisdiction thereof for beverage purposes is hereby prohibited.

Section 2. The Congress and the several States have concurrent power to enforce this article by appropriate legislation.

Section 3. This article shall be inoperative unless it shall have been ratified as an amendment to the Constitution by the legislatures of the several States, as provided in the constitution, within seven years from the date of the submission hereof to the States by the Congress.

RATIFICATION: Jan. 16, 1919

COMMENT: The 18th Amendment created one of this nation's more virulent periods of street violence waged by the then standing groups, criminal enterprises whether referred to as the Mafia, or the "family" or whatever appellation be assigned those who used this ill-conceived prohibition to garner their excessive and illegal profits. It became a preposterous imagery of an overly righteous outcry from certain religious extremists who had determined their sense of morality should become the law of the land. Specific restrictions could have been legislated, state by state. Limitations and additional legal recourse could have been developed, thus minimizing the claimed deleterious effects of rampant alcohol use rather than giving the "mob" a heretofore poorly structured rule for excess and illegal gains.

Its ratification produced a boom in the unlawful and often deadly production of a highly alcoholic brew most commonly referred to "moonshine". Although glorified by the media and the many literary outputs, it was not just the produce of a hill folk only intending to survive economic deprivation. In many instances, the drink was fatal due to its frequent use of less than medically suitable ingredients or processing. Sadly it became more the escutcheon of the moralistic fanatics than any sense of rational need. Today, the sword of prohibition still dominates many local and state legislatures. Driven by religious or hypocritical propriety, it becomes the unsupportable shadow of inability to adjudge appropriate controls and conditions of use that would allow consumption within reason. It is a transparency that can quickly reveal the weakness of pure legislative posturing.

The next Amendment was long in coming, a hundred and forty-four years after the nation's founding. This delay demonstrated more the ongoing chauvinistic attitude of legislators, statewide and nationally, than the lack of recognizing the importance and valued position of the female gender in the success of our country's development. What, in this writer's opinion, is the greatest effect this Amendment has in today's global society, is to announce broadly and most surely that the female is a full co-habiting partner in mankind. That the tribal oriented and basically brutal treatment of and attitude toward females in the Islamic and other Mid-Eastern climes is morally, socially, economically and operationally wrong. It was an evil in our country that was eventually righted. This stature of equality, refused to be recognized by many other countries, is a continuing reflection of the ignorance of many of the world's societies.

•

The 19th Amendment

The right of citizens of the United States to vote shall not be denied or abridged by the United States or by any State on account of sex. Congress shall have the power to enforce this article by appropriate legislation.

RATIFICATION: Aug. 18, 1920

COMMENT: So long the female gender of our nation suffered a debasing absence of any reasonable degree of citizenship when such matters as the right to vote, inherit property, and share in the governance of the country were denied them. As the bearers of the future population, this amendment was not only needed much earlier but was another of the acts of chauvinism perpetrated by a male dominated society. Today, we have become the better for the 19th Amendment in both the equality of all, and the opportunity for advancement now available to our daughters.

Yet disagreement with the supposedly ratified amendment occurred when a suit by qualified voters in Maryland, again referring to Leser v. Garnett, declared the Maryland Board of Registry should strike the names of women from the register of voters on the grounds the state Constitution limited the suffrage to men and thus the 19th amendment was not validly adopted. Again, the Court imposed the principle of *non-delegation* concept as referred to in the 16th Amendment dispute overriding the complaint.

•

The 20th Amendment

COMMENT: The Twentieth Amendment is a lengthy tome, setting the process and conditions under which the terms of the President, Vice President and members of Congress shall function. The succession factor, long in dispute and a contentious element in some past governments, was ostensibly resolved with the line of succession in the instance of a vacancy by inability to serve by death or other circumstances. That included in this order, the President, the Vice President and then the Speaker of the House of Representatives.

Section 1. The terms of the President and Vice President shall end at noon on the 20th day of January, and the terms of Senators and

Representatives at noon on the 3ᵈ day of January, of the years in which such terms would have ended if this article had not been ratified; and the terms of their successors shall then begin.

Section 2. The Congress shall assemble at least once in every year, and such meeting shall begin at noon on the 3ᵈ day of January, unless they shall by law appoint a different day.

Section 3. If, at the time fixed for the beginning of the term of the President, the President elect shall have died, the Vice President elect shall become President. If a President shall not have been chosen before the time fixed for the beginning of his term, or if the President elect shall have failed to qualify, then the Vice President elect shall act as President until a president shall have qualified; and the Congress may by law provide for the case neither a president elect nor a vice president elect shall have qualified, declaring who shall then act as President, or the manner in which one who is to act shall be selected, and such person shall act accordingly until a president or Vice President shall have qualified.

Section 4. The congress may by law provide for the case of the death of any persons from whom the House of Representatives may choose a President whenever the right of choice shall have devolved upon them, and for the case of the death of any of the persons from whom the Senate may choose a vice President whenever the right of choice shall have devolved upon them.

Section 5. Sections 1 and 2 shall take effect on the 15ᵗʰ day of October following ratification of this article.

Section 6. This article shall be inoperative unless it shall have been ratified as an amendment to the Constitution by the legislatures of three-fourths of the several States within seven years from the date of its submission."

RATIFICATION: Jan. 23, 1933

COMMENT: As is common with any verbiage formulated or created by members of the legal profession, Article XX is more confusing at times than content able. Yet, when developed in 1932 it was a difficult task to enumerate succession. Remember, the country had seen three presidents assassinated and one dying shortly after taking office. The assumption of the mantle of executive leadership is an awesome task. It requires a detail that should have simplicity as well as completeness in its presentation. The substance of numerous mystery thrillers, the possible elimination of two or more of the top national executives has repeatedly raised the question in the event of such an occurrence. Who should then be in charge of the most powerful nation on the globe? A rational resolution, in this writer's opinion, has still not been provided the people of this country. A suggested inclusion is here proposed for potential consideration and discussion.

That the presiding officer of the Senate, a duly elected member of that body and being the individual selected by his or her fellow members and being a member of the majority political party in that body, be in line of succession immediately after the Speaker of the House of Representatives. And shall after accession, accept and assume all those duties and responsibilities inherent to the office of the President of the United States for such period as shall remain in the original holder's term of office at the time of succession.

•

The 21st Amendment

Section 1. The eighteenth article of amendment to the Constitution of the United States is hereby repealed.

Section 2. The transportation or importation into any State, Territory, or possession of the United States for the delivery or use therein of intoxicating liquors, in violation of the laws thereof, is hereby prohibited.

Section 3. This article shall be inoperative unless it shall have been ratified as an amendment to the Constitution by conventions in the several States, as provided in the constitution, within seven years from the date of the submissions hereof to the States by the congress.

RATIFICATION: Dec. 5, 1933

COMMENT: The archaic prohibition of intoxicating drink was repealed as it became apparent it did not actually lessen all those evils supposedly perpetuated as constantly proclaimed by the evangelical fervor and fanaticisms of its opponents. However, the states have been allowed to institute their own restrictions, some in rather archaic and excessively puritanical fashion. The creation of "dry" counties or entire states often created stereotypical imagery of backward and socially naïve personas that many of the population in those very areas long felt was both erroneous and damaging to the image of their home location. The right of these local entities to institute such restrictions or laws is the essence of states' rights according to that concept's most ardent supporters. To many, the tax revenue earned from such proliferation of retail availability is a strong reasoning for the removal of such restrictions where possible. The equally strong contention that liberal access leads to excess use remains a principle facet of their position.

The government and its varied constituencies finally recognized that alcoholism is not a human foible that can be legislated. Rather, it is a personal choice that has sent far too many into the depths of self-degradation and suffering that additionally affects the abuser's family and near associates. Proper control of its dispensation is a far better resolution than prohibition. To prohibit can easily propagate the desire to demand its consumption or distribution thus creating potential illegal activities and possibly violence by those choosing to overtly flout the law and engage in competing internecine conflict. To the opposition of the repeal it may incite acceptable personal decisions that can and do, then, lead to excess consumption. If this insistence on the evil of alcohol is mandated by law, it violates the civil rights of the potential partaker. If however, legislated and administered reasonably with reasonable controls it can be an effective function of government.

•

The 22nd Amendment

Section 1. No person shall be elected to the office of the President more than twice, and no person who has held the office of President, or acted as President, for more than two years of a term to which some other person was elected President, shall be elected to the office of president more than once. But this article shall not apply to any person holding the office of President, or acting as President, during the term within which this Article becomes operative from holding the office of president or acting as President during the remainder of such term.

Section 2. This article shall be inoperative unless it shall have been ratified as an amendment to the Constitution by the legislatures of three-fourths of the several States within the seven years from the date of its submission to the States by the Congress."

RATIFICATION: Feb. 27, 1951 (This amendment took the second longest amount of time to ratify: 3 years, 11 months, 6 days.)

COMMENT: In this writer's opinion, this was forwarded to remove the possibility of another three or more term president whose control of that office could mirror the early fears of a potential monarchial format. It does forbid an individual from holding the office after having held that office in accession and then presenting himself or herself for two more four-year terms. However, the inevitable criticisms of a former administration, however biased or seemingly inconsequential, will often diminish if not preclude any individual's influence or personal desire to again mount the global stage as head of currently the most powerful nation in the world.

•

The 23rd Amendment

Section 1. the District constituting the seat of Government of the United States shall appoint in such a manner as Congress may direct: A number of electors of President and vice President equal to the whole number of Senators and Representatives in congress to which the District would be entitled if it were a State, but in no event more than the most populous State; they shall in addition to those appointed by the States, but shall be considered, for the purposes of the election of the President and Vice President, to be electors appointed by a State and they shall meet in the District and perform such duties as provided by the twelfth article of amendment.

Section 2. The congress shall have the power to enforce this article by appropriate legislation.

RATIFICATION: Mar. 29, 1961

COMMENT: This article was ratified in 1961 and has since been at the core of the demands by the population of the District of Columbia to be granted full rights as a State. Demographically and politically, the District is totally controlled by a governing mental set. Majorities of the population are either government employees or are basically dependent on the whims and will of the political party in power at any particular time for those benefits of municipal corporation administration. If granted statehood, the district would then have two Senators and with an appreciable number of Representatives based on population ratio as serves all other states. This could be a potential legislative tool by the party in power to affect decision making in excess of the power held individually by the other fifty states. A dangerous precedent, allowing dominance at times, not envisioned in the structure of the Constitution itself. The demographics of the District are another influence that would present direct pressure in assorted considerations that would again, be counterproductive in the ongoing attempt to maintain a balance in governmental judgment.

•

The 24ᵗʰ Amendment

Section 1. The right of citizens of the United States to vote in any primary or other election for President or Vice President, for electors for President or vice President, or for Senator or Representative in congress, shall not be abridged by the United States or any State by reason of failure to pay poll tax or other tax.

Section 2. The Congress shall have power to enforce this article by appropriate legislation.

RATIFICATION: Jan. 23, 1964

COMMENT: As simple as this recognition and assertion of the citizen's right to vote, the ignominious poll tax and deprivation of a certain part of the populace to vote, particularly in the southern states during the latter part of the 19ᵗʰ Century and the to the mid-20ᵗʰ Century is a regretted part of our history. However, more recently there have been instances of intimidation at the polls as was demonstrated by members of the "Black Panthers" at one or more polling places, which shall be discussed later. In several past elections, manipulation of ballot counts were claimed to have determined the outcome of elections in denial of the voters true wishes. Regardless, the control of election procedure, including security of the voting right, is an obligation of every government in residence at the time of any election. It is the absence of rigid and sufficient application of the right of the citizen to free, uninhibited and open elections that still adds to the less favorable image exhibited by a few major urban areas, particularly in the eastern half of our nation.

The apparent reticence of both the federal law enforcement agencies in recent years to take decisive action against those who would attempt intimidation or delay as refers to immediate and free access to any polling station, is at best a violation of their oath to uphold the rule of law. It calls to mind the inequities and insufficiencies of such protection of the citizen's right that were so prevalent not that many years ago.

•

The 25th Amendment

Section 1. In case of removal of the president from office or his death or resignation, the vice president shall become president.

Section 2. Whenever there is a vacancy in the office of the vice president, the president shall nominate a vice president who shall take office upon confirmation by a majority of both Houses of Congress.

Section 3. Whenever the President transmits to the President pro tempore of the Senate and the Speaker of the House of Representatives his written declaration that he is unable to discharge the powers and duties of his office, and until he transmits them a written declaration to the contrary, such powers and duties shall be discharged by the vice President as Acting President.

Section 4. whenever the Vice President and a majority of either the principal officers of the executive departments or of such other body as Congress may proscribe by law provide, transmits to the President pro tempore of the Senate and the Speaker of the House of Representatives their written declaration that the President is unable to discharge the powers and duties of his office, the vice President shall immediately assume the powers and duties of the office as Acting President.

Thereafter, when the President transmits to the President pro tempore of the Senate and the Speaker of the House of Representatives that no inability exists, he shall resume the powers and duties of his office unless the vice president and a majority of either the principal officers of the executive department or of such body as Congress may by law provide, transmit within four days to the President pro tempore of the Senate and the Speaker of the House of Representatives their written declaration that the President is unable to discharge the powers and duties of his office. Thereupon Congress shall decide the issue, assembling within forty-eight hours for that purpose if not in session. If Congress, within twenty-one days after receipt of the latter written declaration, or, if Congress not in session, within twenty-one days after Congress is required to assemble, determines by two-thirds vote of both Houses that the president is unable to discharge the powers and duties of his office, the Vice President shall continue to discharge the same as Acting President; otherwise, the President shall resume the powers and duties of his office."

RATIFICATION: Feb. 10, 1967

COMMENT: As convoluted as it may appear, it merely reflects the nature of the legal profession's desire to exalt their use of the English language. Furthermore, it can placate those who find simplicity a work of the plebian masses and insist on pursuing their own verbal meandering. Although ostensibly already restated by the enacted succession rule generated by Congress in recent years, would it not be clearer in intent and process to say the following?

"That upon the medically and legally based conclusion of those assigned that responsibility and such documented conclusion agreed to by a two-thirds vote of both Houses as to the inability of the President to

continue execution of his or her duties and powers, the Vice-President shall assume the powers and duties of that office until a determination as to return to office by the President is concurred with by a majority of both Houses.

In the event of the death of the sitting President or his or her total disability to continue the duties and powers of that office during the foreseeable conclusion of the term for which that individual was elected to serve, the Vice-President shall assume the duties and powers of the Presidency. In such instance, he or she shall continue in that position until the end of the term for which the deceased or disabled holder was elected to serve.

Were the Vice-President to be deceased or unable to pursue his or her duties and powers of that office, the Speaker of the House, currently serving, shall assume the position of the Vice-President until the end of the term for which the Vice-President was elected or until that person, disabled, can return to full execution of the powers and duties of that office.

Upon rising to the position of Vice-President, the then Speaker of the House shall relinquish all of his or her powers and duties as are prescribed for that position and the membership of the House of Representatives shall select a replacement by no less than a two-thirds vote of those currently elected to that body and being members of the majority political party in that body at that time. In the event of that body being in recess or not in session for whatever reason, it shall be required that they shall meet and so select the replacement for the Speaker of the House position with a period of no less than seventy-two hours. And furthermore, the newly elected Speaker shall then assume the position of third in line of succession to the presidency as is so prescribed herein."

Here again, the succession route has been detailed previously, but not in the firm and less revocable law of the Constitution. Without this type of etched detail, it is possible for one or more political groups, gaining control of either House of Congress, to determine preferential alignment for the purposes of succession to the highest office in the land. Also, you will note I have added "his or her" since in the not too distant future, the female gender will, in my opinion, grace the White House as our nation's Chief Executive. Additionally, this writer has earlier suggested another inclusion into that line of succession.

●

The 26th Amendment

Section 1. The right of citizens of the United States, who are eighteen years of age or older, to vote shall not be denied or abridged by the United States of any State on account of age.

Section 2. The congress shall have power to enforce this article by appropriate legislation."

RATIFICATION: July 1, 1971. (This amendment took the shortest time to ratify, 3 months, 8 days.)

COMMENT: This has been bantered and verbally mauled for years. We can send our youths to war, require their compliance with many laws but deny them the right to help select our national leadership. Because of the gap between age eighteen and twenty-one, they were considered ill fit to accept and exercise this most treasured right of a citizen. Well phrased if I do say so myself. But with this allocation of rights and permission to be a part of the country they have often died defending, today, has arisen an embarrassing fact relating to those newly enfranchised youth. It was only several decades ago that young people crowded the streets protesting war—the Vietnam crisis—perceived or contended injustices by local or national government. They screamed out their protest, often in violent action or expletive laden language. They demanded equal rights and their voice in the future makeup of our legislative bodies. Their mentors, the hollow proponents of youthful rights, often proclaimed from the stage at drug fueled frenetic music concerts, did little to prepare their young constituency as to the true responsibility of rational execution of that right.

However, today we will sadly read the statistics on the youth vote, particularly the 18 to 30 age range. Their presence at the polling locations, whether it be a local municipal election or statewide or the ever present congressional and quadrennial elections, their participation ranks just below the desire to stand and watch grass grow. Their reticence or inattentiveness to this so valued right has made a mockery of the attempts by those long demanding equality at the polls for that younger constituency.

In order to provide substance to this voting franchise, the younger generation must spend less time vocalizing in TV coverage prompted demonstrations and a greater time being prepared to vote responsibly. Protesting is one form of demanding change. But the voting booth is far more powerful in altering the reasons for dissent. Yet, first, it would behoove them and all concerned to learn sufficiently, the elements of the Constitution and the history of our founding that provided them this great privilege and the process for selecting our leadership as is included therein.

It is the opinion of the writer that a necessary corollary to the teachings of the Constitution throughout the educational process from initial discussion through the highest levels should be the insistence that the student exercise his or her right to vote in every pertinent election whatever their personal avowed position on the subjects of the day. That to avoid this right and privilege of citizenship is to totally ignore the importance of being taught the rights and even more so the obligations of enjoying the freedoms provided in our Constitution and accompanying laws.

•

The 27th Amendment

No law, carrying compensation for the services of the Senators and Representatives, shall take effect, until an election of representation shall have intervened.

RATIFICATION: May 7, 1992 (This amendment was first proposed on Sept.1, 1789, making it the amendment that took the longest time to be ratified: 202 years, 7 months and 12 days.)

COMMENT: Basically it says "don't get any ideas about raising your salaries and increasing the associated perks above what is stipulated during your time in Congress". I would suggest this addition to this Amendment as follows:

"Beyond the stated wage as referred to herein, a detailed list of those services from which public funds are used, shall be a part of the public record and reviewed with the inauguration of each new Congressional session within a time frame of no less than two years. And that a record of repayment for such services and which have been provided without reimbursement, be made a part of the public record and herewith publicized by the media on a yearly basis and prior to any period of election of any and all members of both Houses of Congress."

The "perks" or benefits provided members of Congress, far exceed those in the private sector. It should be a rule that Congress equally abide by all laws they impose on all American people. That a close examination of the benefits be reviewed each four year period to assure they are neither excessive or fall below the average that other Americans receive or enjoy. Most egregious is the massive health benefits and outrageous pension plan enjoyed by members of Congress, many receiving them for only a few years in office. Possibly their pay could be raised by approximately twenty-five per-cent. Then they would be required to purchase their own health plan and become part of the national social security plan as do we all. Finally, Congress could stipulate in advance their planned vacation periods, no period to last longer than three weeks or occur more than three times during the calendar year.

● ● ●

● ● ●

RECAP "ONE"

Now that we've washed this venerable document, rinsed it and hung it out to dry, lets fold its four corners. In this writer's opinion, the structure of this virtual blanket that covers our personal and societal liberties is comprised of the seven Articles that precede the amendments covered earlier in this dissertation. Without excessive repetition regarding the many elements contained therein, I will refer to only specific portions of sections in each of those Articles seeming most in need of further comment.

The writer now takes the opportunity to address three subjects that the current and past several national administrations may have seemed powerless or less than competent to address, whether fully or substantively. They have appeared to slumber while the eventual need to compromise and achieve legislative resolution concerning the many subjects faced or initiated by the Congress is the paramount purpose of their position. It is a blockage that subverts the original intent of our Founding Fathers and later proponents of the amendments to further the interests of a free society with definitive and worthwhile lawmaking.

Article I – Section 1 - All legislative powers contained herein granted shall be vested in a Congress of the United States, which shall consist of a Senate and House of Representatives.

COMMENT: What is contained within this section has formed the present upheaval in public demand for a return to stronger local and states' rights. It has promulgated such opposing groups as the somewhat disparate "Tea Party" movement. It was expected by many that the 9th and 10th Amendments would and should resolve any such conflict between the rights of the national administration and the states that constitute the nation as a whole. However, such has not occurred. Each political party, upon taking power, and after declaring their steadfast belief in the rights of the individual citizen and the states, immediately move to dictate changes in norms and traditions, once felt inviolable by the citizenry. It is this philosophical and human conduct diagnosis that is not the purview of elected representatives.

The use of Executive Orders has become in recent years, ostensibly a tool by whomever resides in the White House to defy any opposition by the Congress to that individual's avowed intent to implement legislation and regulation normally the role of legislature. These powers are invested in legislatively mandated positions and legal acceptance, not the control of single entities answerable only to one individual, regardless of that person's level of power or influence. A paradigm that exists within any legislative body is that they must assure their constituents they are acting only in their best interests and that their attempts to adjust social norms and traditional social conduct is not intrusive. Rather, performed as a protective measure to assure the good of the people.

The sovereignty of the state as opposed to the overall responsibilities of the federal government is at the core of the debate. The conflict between the national government's attempt to maintain and, under various administrations, increase their power to regulate and the individual states' claim to those rights enumerated in the constitution is a battle never to be won but assuredly one that will divide politically and economically.

Section 8 – (repeated)
"...to pay the debts and provide for the common Defence and general Welfare of the United States;" and ". . . To borrow Money on the credit of the United States;"

COMMENT: And here we have the purposed power to create and enact entitlements through which the horrendous national debt is now strained to a near breaking point almost surpassing the ability and capacity of this country to repay the billions borrowed from foreign countries. Some of those countries are formerly avowed enemies of our way of life. Yet today, our economy is in a strangle hold to these global creditors, who could, in concert with one another, fiscally bring our country's financial institution to its knees. And possibly force us to make commitments and relinquish our position, militarily and fiscally in certain very sensitive parts of the world. Nuclear concern has become far less threatening than the monetary monster our constant borrowing has created.

"To establish a uniform Rule of Naturalization,"

COMMENT: Again, this reflects a required duty which past administrations from the mid-20th Century to the present, have butchered as to maintaining and accomplishing what our Founding Fathers may have meant. In the past several decades, national administrations and legislatures have floundered in their own whirlpool of petty bickering or regrettably just possible incompetent compliance with existing immigration and access laws concerning those wishing to enter the United States. What is needed is an extensive review of those immigration and access laws and regulations now in effect. Winnowing out the unnecessary and implementing the firm rules of visitation by foreign individuals is the critical first step. Then, a plan to allow certain added benefits to those legally desiring access to our shores, but with a strongly worded and definitive set of obligations and rights by law enforcement at local, state and national levels to assure appropriate compliance with those laws and conditions of access.

The constant wrangling between those who want direct and firm compliance with the immigration process, and the more liberal element who want the borders open without restriction has reached a deafening roar. We must institute a method of fair and substantive vetting of all those seeking access to what has become the last bastion of a free people.

● ● ●

● ● ●

RECAP "TWO"

COMMENT: There are still elements of our government's administration which I feel need to institute a more disciplined approach to providing the services and assistance to the national constituency. This is particularly evident in the mass of officialdom who continually either resist or are immune from the normal business practice of either reducing or eliminating personnel, however high their position might be, when found to be lacking in competency or responsibility for the failures in proper oversight including actions by their subordinates. Nonsuccess through insufficiency of talent or effort is not excusable regardless of political or social position. It denies the populace a fair and equitable effort that even if unsuccessful should not be ignored or absolved of blame when insufficiency of effort or inappropriate action is the evident fault. Again, this is the personal opinion of the writer but one which he feels is shared by many others and must be more openly discussed, regardless of the reticence of a biased media to publicly explore the issues as follows. We are all responsible for our personal and professional actions regardless of status or difficulties that confront us.

1. The Immigration & Customs Enforcement (ICE) & Homeland Security

COMMENT: The ICE and its oversight cabinet post have torn the nation apart by allowing an insufficiency in holding firm our borders. They are lax in attending to obvious violations and refuse to admit their incompetency by relegating any complaint to political bantering. Previous administrations cannot claim any notable ability to control illegal entry. But during the past several decades all three branches of the government have exacerbated the situation with their inactivity and political posturing. Until ordered debate and constructive compromise comes forth from both Houses of Congress and is accepted by a president putting aside his or her political ambition, we will continue to wander on an endless sea of conflict in word and action. The lack of definitive and direct action by the prior administration and the more recent and strongly decried Executive Orders by the currently seated President, has added increased woes and difficulties for all border agents. Among this flow of the undocumented and the present resident population of over eleven million illegally accessed individuals, many from south of our nation's border, Mexico, Central and South America, some others in 'refugee' status, have been many criminals and feared adherents to the virulent Islamic Jihadist ideology. It is a sensitive subject that cannot be resolved with rhetoric however well-meant or at times seemingly vitriolic. It is a situation only action, due process and well define process can correct. It is true we are an amalgamation of the most ethnically and culturally diverse population on the globe. And from this potpourri of personalities and social, economic and definitely political viewpoints will always cause division in thought regardless of demands by many for unity of position.

2. The Office of the Attorney General of the United States

COMMENT: This office was envisioned as carrying forth the needs of the citizenry in pursuing those rights and protecting those liberties enumerated in the Constitution. Its obligation is to be non-partisan as concerning a relationship with the Judicial and Legislative branches. However, it also must be the guardian of equal representation and uniform application of current law. The disavowal of their obligation to seek legal restraint and prosecution of the filmed Black Panther members intimidating incoming voters at one of the polls in the 2008 presidential election violated that office's oath. It shamed both the office and the Executive Branch of which it is a part. But again, it too has been politicized to an embarrassing degree.

The office has regrettably become in the past years merely another political prize and endangers the very concept of protection of the constitution over all other regards, political or military. In addition, the preemptory involvement vocally into several major police related incidents, moved the balance of justice expected from that office well beyond the pale of reasonable concern into the murky depths of bias. It is an area of social interface that they have spent far too much effort to instigate self-aggrandizing rather than a purposeful and effective interrelationship to help correct the evident problems with certain aspects of local law enforcement's relationship to the public it serves.

3. The National Law Enforcement and Intelligence Services

COMMENT: Here we have seen an ongoing turf war. Like small children squabbling over the ownership of toys they forget they do not own—those functions being the obligations they have sworn to uphold and execute in the most effective manner allowable—too often in recent years they have forgotten they are paid by the citizenry to enjoin, to combat and to bring to adjudication, criminal acts and any attempts to attack or illegally influence the stability of our country domestically and abroad. Repeatedly, information, critical to the defense of this country against our enemies, is withheld by one group in the desire to have total control. The tragedy of September 11, 2001, the "Cole naval vessel assault", the Oklahoma City Federal Courthouse bombing; the list is endless. These are prime examples of small minded individuals using acquired information about latent, serious situations to feather their own nest with self-aggrandizement. And more so, to prohibit other agencies the opportunity to share in the laudatory that comes with successful elimination or forestalling of such potential threats. Until all these mandated agencies, the FBI, CIA, NSC, NSA, ICE, ATF, DEA and the IRS, a truly self-aggrandizing menagerie of turf guarding sycophants are forced to interrelate and share information on a broad scale, this "being unprepared" mentality will continue.

4. The Rule of Law in All Our Courts

COMMENT: Some have suggested that Sharia Law might have a basis in considering various cases wherein its use would be a fair adjudication of certain matters involving those of the Islamic persuasion. Sharia law can never be countenanced by any court in the United States or its controlled territories or any outlying geographical aspects who might be later considered for membership within the protection and administration of this country. Any society that requires individual liberty as a prerequisite for stability and advancement of the common interest, must deny and prohibit the institution or even the simplest acceptance of the most commonly benign parts of Sharia Law into our legal and judicial systems. It would be, in this writer's strongest opinion, an absolute and total violation of basic Constitutional rights. It serves the perverted sense of discipline expressed in many theocratic and ideologically controlled areas of the earth. And like any disease, it must be stopped from transmission before its invidious nature is communicated into any part of our judicial system.

Sharia Law is the declaration of required subjugation of the masses. It is based on a tribal dominance that has existed since the earliest days of Islamic history. But, more recently it has become the insistence of the Islamic movement. Too often, at the point of a sword, the weapon's trigger and the devastating nature of human bomb carriers. It has no place in our legal lexicon. Regardless of any less offensive or ostensibly moderate portions, Sharia law is an enemy to the assured equality of everyman appearing before the bar of justice and must be kept at bay and if attempts to infiltrate our judicial considerations continue, it must be immediately countermanded in the most effective manner possible.

5. An Abomination; the Civil Litigation Process

COMMENT: The right of the citizen to seek redress in civil court, unhindered by authoritarian control exercised in many other countries is one of the basic freedoms that should be enjoyed by the citizenry. However, for years, the American judicial system has found little need to expedite such litigations involving various claims for reimbursement, civil actions regarding injury or death and the many other reasons for seeking judicial review. Can not a more speedy and efficient process be developed. A suggested format could possibly involve the following criteria:

a) An immediate preliminary hearing to determine if there is substantive legal basis for the proffered litigation to proceed. If lacking merit or without stable legal reasoning, the case would then be referred to later dockets. E.g. the hundreds of miscellaneous and nuisance suits filed yearly.

b) When solid legal basis is found to exist for either party, an appropriate date for another preliminary hearing should be set with proper and sufficient documentation presented revealing the fundamental controversy or differences in position.

c) Once that is determined a date is then set with predetermined and reasonable time frame set during which the matter is held and/or resolved. Failure to be prepared or action to delay by additional claims and/or legal maneuvers shall cause an immediate hearing to determine if such actions or moves by either party, are meant or intended or appear to be methods to deny or diminish the right of redress by one party to the detriment of the other. Too often, legal wrangling and the clever manipulation of the appeals and submission of additional claims and documentation have been used by the more affluent party to decimate the position of the less financially advantaged party. When such lack of fiscal resources or sufficient legal counsel or proven inappropriate delay or hindrance forces either party into submission, the judicial system and the rights under the First Amendment are being violated.

d) When a judgment has been reached or a settlement concluded, one of the major flaws in the legal process is the delay in paying the successful party in any such litigation. Regardless of the right to appeal and its often lengthy time span, the awarded sum should be placed in court supervised and controlled escrow until the appeals process is completed. Today, many have been victors in their litigated position but must either wait years for any payment, or find that time and endless delays preclude their ever receiving adjudged compensation or award.

6. The quadrennial presidential race.

COMMENT: Every four years we engage in a combination Brazilian

Carnival, New Orleans famed Mardi Gras and an adult Woodstock reunion. At the early stages of this writing, a major candidate for that office had utilized a supposed foundation she and her husband control, to acquire donations from various foreign governments and highly suspect activist groups from outside our country. Now, determined so far as not to be illegal, it still increases the stench of conflict of interest and unethical pandering for funds to become the world leader who would later be dealing with those same donors. I would suggest the following requirement of all presidential candidates, regardless of political connection or level of potential success in forthcoming primaries or the general election:

"That all income, funding, donations, whether personal, party connected, or through any type of PAC or like organization, that may either come directly from a foreign government, agency or activist group or individual citizen of that country, be made a part of the public record and said information available to both the media and political opponents of the recipient candidate within thirty days of such funding. As for the general election, said information must be revealed no less than sixty days prior to the date of said general election."

It would be preferable that dates set for primary caucuses and public voting, once set, should remain in status so as to allow potential candidates to appropriately prepare. In this writer's years of viewing this quadrennial circus, such mature and rational consideration will never occur as long as the possible accession to the world's most powerful leadership retains its mesmerizing lure. Thus, strike up the band and unfurl the banners, the big show will go on.

● ● ●

● ● ●

Future Vigilance

The U.S. Constitution, as a noble representation of human rights and the desires of man to be free, is still a document that needs continual reviewing. First should be the reconstitution of the understanding by its citizens as to the intent of its writers. And next, to assure it continues to reflect those liberties as definitive of our nature as a free people. With this review in mind, do these comments require a constitutional convention? Eventually, perhaps but not with the heretofore activist public groups demand for immediate change with little time for consideration.

Needed first is a nonpartisan commission, devoid of political figures, comprised of members of commerce, religious groups, social activist groups who are not tied to existing political parties or known proponents of demagoguery. This will not be easy to accomplish, but is absolutely necessary. Then, after a review of those issues most complainant by citizen and recognized activist groups, then and only then, should a menu of possible considerations be presented to Congress for their review and vote as to enabling a constitutional conclave. It would be at such a Constitutional convention that pertinent and definitive recommendations can be put forward to fulfill the format for presentation to the states for their review and vote. After that, the rule of change can take place, unhindered and unaffected by the desire of political ideologies to delay or infect with the virus of personal agendas. If this can occur every decade or so, one can then submit logically that the Constitution is a living document.

A postscript if you would. We need to recognize a major flaw that exists in this expedition into the verbiage of the Constitution. As a youngster in a rural school, we were by the sixth grade, expected to be informed of the various elements of the Constitution. In fact, we studied the basic tenets of that document as it existed at that time. Included was the wording and meaning of the Declaration of Independence, the preamble to the Constitution and its articles and Amendments. It was not imposed on us as superfluous dialogue but rather, as a required understanding of the foundation of our form of government. And more importantly, it provided individual freedoms many of our ancestors and current relatives have suffered their lives to preserve during WW II and the ensuing conflicts.

It was considered critical that we understood the core of the Constitution so as to be better able to become intelligent voters, those who would choose our future electors. Today, it is lamentable that any such instruction is rare if even practiced to any measurable degree. Each spring we spit out students, ill prepared to deal with the polyglot nature of the body politics and rule of law constantly debated and challenged in today's society.

Sadly, our younger generations are set adrift in the miasma of a continuing ignorance of our national beginnings. Regrettable, but too true, any basic instruction that may occur in the lower grades will be instantly bastardized within and tainted by the liberal, tenure controlled, ivory towers of advanced academia such as major institutions; the renowned Harvard, the venerable Princeton and Yale, and the equally leftist oriented Columbia University, who will immediately begin a concentrated attack on those traditional beliefs held by the majority of the populace. The Constitution will be derided, change for any myriad reason demanded. Students will leave such institutions of higher learning to believe what they've been taught earlier is a façade behind which an evil premise lies.

What this writer fears is a continuing decline of instructional objectivity. It can create young graduates who are sure they have heard the final and most effective viewpoint relative to the government and the social structure as exists at the time of their graduation. It is like a coming wind, blowing hard against brick walls of current and long held concepts, only to realize that sufficient education is in reality the door to careful thought, logical reflection and reasonable compromise through which new ideas advance. I am a firm believer that academic tenure, when administered judiciously is important to maintaining the quality of instruction we expect of our institutions of higher learning. It allows research and writings to expound on individual theories and hopefully expands the general knowledge of the individual academic's personal efforts. Yet, tenure, forced on academic institutions by self-gratifying employee unions, has created demagogues who under this protective mantle, have attempted to radicalize the less informed and very impressionable collegians. Yet we continue to elect the district and state educational officials who serve as pimps providing these unions their unseemly and improper control.

Today, as it did in the 18th Century, and has through the two hundred plus years of our existence, the Constitution has changed in a legally and ethically determined manner. However, the substance of the Constitution must remain the sole discretion of the citizenry. Otherwise, we could become a polymorphous society. We would become unable to maintain a consistent policy and direction in our unending desire to keep those freedoms we have striven so hard to attain. It should be remembered that the written word is a monument to man's creativity that the winds and vagaries of time can never wear away or diminish from recorded history. Words are the enduring legacy of anyone observing the passing parade of human evolution. Many words have been uttered and today increase in volume and frequency through the ever expanding electronic media. However, vocal declarations can be lost to memory and as often repeated, can be ever changed in meaning and interpretation. The U.S. Constitution is a standing monument to man's intent to provide a better life for those it embraced, allowing the pure dissident or the irrational advocate to instill their personal agendas within the wording without restraint.

For many, the greatest protection to assuring the solidarity of constitutional interpretation is the Supreme Court – the highest judicial body in these United States. That, according to the original concept of the then new governmental structure as decided by the Founding Fathers stipulated that three distinct entities—Executive, Legislative and Judicial—shall be and are consecrated to be equal but separate functions.

This is a myth far too long foisted on the citizenry. Associate U.S. Supreme Court Justice Antonin Scalia wrote in a 1997 essay, "A Matter of Interpretation"–"Judges in short become lawmakers". Further, in the summer of a year 2000 speech, he said, "The fundamental danger in a democratic society is that excessive and overly expanded judicial power tends to rob the people of the ability to decide for themselves how they would live and within what kind of society they would dwell."

So let us address the principle question regarding our judicial system at all levels. What is the basic mission of judicial interpretation and review? Is it to correct or redirect the standards of social conduct and human activity for future generations? Or is it to maintain the structure of the laws as they currently exist and to purge our operational system of any and all regulations that would deny or limit the freedoms granted each citizen by the Constitution? We constantly hear of demands for justice from what is considered by some as a tyrannical administration of the law or regulatory power exerted by Congress or the Executive Branch. Contrary to the desire of many to limit protest, which too often has been scenes of more violent action, there still remains a simple inquiry. Can we bar any person from passing a message, however phrased or publicly staged when seeking or searching for redress? This is a right ostensibly assured in the First Amendment.

The Executive Branch can often be held hostage by a legislature of opposing political and economic aims. Even the veto power of the President has been weakened by the numerous rules of parliamentary process that beggars the imagination. Control is the product of power, and with its accompanying strength allows those who can and will, to maintain that control. It is, however, required that those seeking such control and exhibiting power must first unite each element of the society to conforming its disparate views within a codified doctrine. This would be a common acceptance of domination that has never been the ilk of most Americans. When that sense of entitled control reaches into the Executive Branch, corruption begins at the highest level. Anyone in the position as globally powerful as the Presidency of the United States, considering him or herself enfranchised to dominate the legislative system and administration of the Constitution, he or she becomes a fabricated dictator. This can never be allowed.

This writer firmly believes that within the original concept that brought forth the Constitution and its resulting Amendments and changes, the will of the people was to be supreme. That no singular person or group are supposed to rule. Rather, the constituency chooses a certain number of their group to administer the affairs of the state – not to rule. The struggle of the law as it is and the government as it wishes to be, remains an eternal battle. The Rule of Law is the adhesive that binds ever tenuously this loosely woven fabric of society in which we currently exist. It is our gift to our children at a price they can never repay. The philosopher Cicero wrote that the good of the people is the chief law. To our legislators and other elected officials wherever they may reside, from hamlet to metropolis, there is a marked difference between knowing the law and understanding its purpose in the judicial process. Knowing the law requires the ability to recite the verbiage and existing form. To understand the law is to recognize its reasoning and its exercise when called upon to resolve any question of conduct or omission. It has long been said that the law should be neither master nor vassal of the constituency it intends to serve.

Justice Lord Hugh L. Markby, a member of the then British controlled Indian High Court, wrote in his 1868 volume "The Elements of Law"; "The value of law lies not in the happiness it creates, but rather the misery and suffering it prevents." A more recent viewpoint was enumerated in the 2002 book, "First Among Equals" by noted jurist Kenneth Starr. He voiced, "The process of judging tends to be highly 'subjective".

Young law students are first immersed in the depths and never ending verbiage of common law, whether contract or tort affecting business, commerce, human conduct and individual liberties which are contended to aid or be injurious to persons or given policies. What is seemingly missing is an understanding of how changes in the law are too often reflective of human nature, the innate bigotry of an insecure judiciary, too influenced by political or personal reasoning. Mankind has no greater voice than the laws that govern its existence.

Thomas Jefferson wrote that "Prudence, indeed will dictate that governments long established should not be changed for light and transient causes; and accordingly all experience hath shown that mankind are more disposed to suffer while evils are sufferable, than to right themselves by abridging the forms to which they are accountable."

It is this caution that must shadow every desired and proposed change. We are not adversarial animals by nature but rather beings. It was this human desire to strive in the face of opposition or dissent by others that provided the will and strength of our forebears to survive and eventually succeed. But is it not the purpose of the Constitution to keep fundamental rights out of the reach of the government? To distance from the kings of old the power and intent to personally control that aspect of human destiny for which they have no right, whether politically or divinely inspired?

Before the more liberal reader considers my earlier remarks regarding the growing entitlement situation as being bigoted, allow me to clarify any seeming misrepresentation. We will always have an impoverished group, those unable or by non-instigated situations who require the assistance of public provision. It is only those who would misuse the purpose of required welfare sustenance that I point to as creating the fiscal abyss that causes lack of necessary funding for the qualified needy and the image of greed the system's critics will use as political fodder.

To the novice researcher or first-timer pursuing a closer look at the Constitution, always remember several important facets of the document.

- It was written in a language almost extinct in style from today's common vernacular and slang.
- It must be respected for its intent at that time and not as an antiquated novelty.
- Look for the substance rather than as a grammar which has evolved over the past several centuries.

With this in mind, one can find fascinating insight within its segments and hopefully, a clearer view of how our nation was instituted and its opportunities for a brighter future. Those who insist the good of one segment of the populace has preeminent value to the constituted freedom of the all are the architects of eventual loss of such freedoms by all.

Change will come in those relevant issues requiring a more rational approach. But, it should be remembered by those too anxious to alter, that all living forms fear and react to change in differing ways. Yet it can only be accomplished through the attention of a population lettered in the basic premises of the Constitution. An understanding that must begin in the elementary years of our youth's educational process. Without that early instruction, later consideration becomes merely the babbling of the uninformed.

The United States Constitution was the first and only document to explicitly define, and declare paramount the position of the citizen in the structure of the government emplaced. It was the initial removal by an encompassed citizenry from their previous controlling force. Like many other attempts throughout history, it took violence in the form of physical resistance and the loss of life on both sides of the issue. However, unlike so many others, it was the intent and the successful fulfillment or our predecessor's objective that after the inevitable conflict there arose a substantial formation of the type of general freedom they'd envisioned. It marked the institution of free expression that has resonated around the globe for over two hundred and thirty years; the echo of which has seemingly died through hypocrisy. Yet I've given even more thought as to how this insignificant speck in a massive hierarchy of stars and other astral bodies ever came to be. This writer is not overtly religious, but I believe strongly in recognizing and allowing full expression by those whose theological and ideological bent is an important part of their understanding of the constitutional freedoms as they've been taught or appropriately informed.

What I've always questioned is why we are here in the manner we reflect today? From the fossil fragments found in some dusty gulch, hidden from view for millennia, we are supposed to have determined our rising from bacterial minutia to technological heights enjoyed today and unimagined just a few centuries ago. I have little understanding of the "big bang theory". Possibly, it may have just been God coughing billions of years ago. Yet, religion in speech or action or demand for specific rights, makes the judiciary very nervous. Law enforcement fears treading too firmly in that area and thus creates conflict in interpretation when none should exist.

The reader will note I've referred to Thomas Jefferson numerous times. Not that he was the sole genesis of the document referred to herein. More recently his history which dubious pedagogues have highlighted his slave holding, like his many colleagues of the time and a somewhat controversial relationship with one of those female slaves cannot be used to disdain the brilliance of thought encompassed in the essential concept of the Declaration of Independence. Rather, it was his initial words and later his interposing of various reflections that have become standard interpretations by academics and political voices throughout the past 200 plus years. There will be those to claim that his pronouncements must be viewed through a somewhat shaded glass. That his ownership of slaves reduces his stature among the nation's historic icons.

To those who may contest the use of his words, please remember, Jefferson was the first to introduce a bill banning slavery upon his entry to the Colonial Virginia Legislature. It failed as did his later proposal again in the national legislature when that body was eventually formed. To say any one viewpoint is the sole source for final analysis is to be misled by refusing to look beyond the linguistic borders existing today.

The United States Constitution is the finest document espousing free spirit and equality of all its participants ever devised; hewed from the forests of thought and concern that arose from a people's desire to be one in themselves and together as a group in a like-thinking society. With the very possible change in direction regarding many present political, economic, and social policies through a new national administration and control of both houses by the same party, one only hope that what is in the best of the populace will be the basis of all such decisions. However, remember words are not as clear as the crystal but rather are shrouded by a lusterless veil aiding the interpretative intent of the viewer.

As this overlook by an average citizen was being written, our national administration changed, as is possible every quadrennial presidential election moment. It was not the intent of the writer to include or integrate any of the current political discourse and ensuring arguments among various entities regarding problems or situations they may feel demand immediate resolution. What the next few years will portend, is neither in the ability nor potential lifespan of the writer to present. The forces of discord that have marked the evolution of our current political environment will, unless tempered by reason and public outcry, continue to create havoc in the legislative process and chaos in the administration of this great nation. There is regrettably a seemingly non-ending ideological conflict between the ultra-left and extremist right and an equal disparity in opinion regarding the media's participation and/or responsibility in the public presentation of public comment whether it be accusatory or rebuttal.

Termism, both on the international scene and the domestic violence experience here, has shaken the domestic calm that so many in the odder age group had come to believe was our tradition and severely frightened the younger generations, causing a national fear of the impending and unknown tomorrow. Still, the Constitution is that bedrock of personal liberty that should not be allowed to be undermined by the recent spate of social and political unrest or demands for instantaneous change in its content – change only to satisfy social or political faddism.

The inevitable inquiry is: should there be held a constitutional convention to respond to these demands?

To some, that is a solid method to update that venerable document in order to clarify certain heretofore contentious or often misunderstood provisos. For the more polar/fringe minded of us it would become an opportunity to correct or nullify all their proclaimed deficiencies and bring that ageless instrument into what is declared modern times. The fear of the opposition is that such a convention will become a cacophony of controversial concepts and ideological demagoguery; that what is today considered less than controlled, would become even more in disarray.

The future of the Constitution is in the hands of those with whom we may have little insight as to their philosophical, political, ethical or social nature. We can only hope that if and when such a conclave occurs it will bring reason and moderation to the table, successful in its results and leave dissonance to those who care less about anything offered except what they propose. It is here I leave the reader. The next step is up to you and your successors.

Finis!

● ● ●

ABOUT THE AUTHOR

James Oshust's fifty year career included executive management of major entertainment, sports and exposition facilities; participation in management roles for the 1996 & 2002 Olympic Games, 1994 World Cup Soccer Championships and the 1998 TBS sponsored "Goodwill Games." Additionally, as an executive with one of the initial professional soccer clubs in the United Sates and facility design and event operations consultant with over forty projects domestically and abroad including two other Olympic Games. He is the author of three novels. He and his wife Barbara, a former professional ice skater and recognized artist reside in Salt Lake City, Utah.

www.ingramcontent.com/pod-product-compliance
Lightning Source LLC
Chambersburg PA
CBHW051057250726
48656CB00001B/333